PERSISTENT

BUSINESS, INVESTMENTS AND LIFE.

BRETT CHRISTOPHER LEMOS

© **Copyright 2020 - All rights reserved.**

The content contained within this book may not be reproduced, duplicated, or transmitted without direct written permission from the author or the publisher.

Under no circumstances will any blame or legal responsibility be held against the publisher, or author, for any damages, reparation, or monetary loss due to the information contained within this book, either directly or indirectly.

Legal Notice:

This book is copyright protected. It is only for personal use. You cannot amend, distribute, sell, use, quote or paraphrase any part, or the content within this book, without the consent of the author or publisher.

Disclaimer Notice:

Please note the information contained within this document is for educational and entertainment purposes only. All effort has been executed to present accurate, up to date, reliable, complete information. No warranties of any kind are declared or implied. Readers acknowledge that the author is not engaged in the rendering of legal, financial, medical, or professional advice. The content within this book has been derived from various sources. Please consult a licensed professional before attempting any techniques outlined in this book.

By reading this document, the reader agrees that under no circumstances is the author responsible for any losses, direct or indirect, that are incurred as a result of the use of the information contained within this document, including, but not limited to, errors, omissions, or inaccuracies.

CONTENTS

Introduction	5
1. Business Basics, Delivery	13
2. Business, Advanced concepts	34
3. Real Estate, your home and others.	48
4. Stocks, 401k, ETFs, Bonds, REITS and Gold and Silver.	79
5. College, courses and online businesses	96
6. Recessions, Depressions, Pandemics	111
7. Sales, in Business and Life.	125
8. Govt. Bailouts, SBA loans, PPP, and EIDL	144
9. Crypto, Bitcoin: The Future of a Bubble	152
10. Pensions	176
11. Life	184
Conclusion	193
Glossary	201
Resources	209

LIST OF 4 MAJOR BASICS I HAD BEFORE SUCCESS

The last thing we want is for you to not have your basics in to succeed.

HONESTLY FOR THIS BOOK TO WORK YOU WILL NEED THESE 4 BASICS.

TO RECEIVE YOUR FREE 4 MAJOR BASICS LIST, VISIT THE LINK BELOW.

www.brettlemos.com

INTRODUCTION

Welcome to my book!

Now I would like to identify and state the problem a lot of people, possibly like yourself have had--- trouble Winning in business, investing and in general, *life*.

PERSISTING has everything to do with winning. If it's a worthwhile goal/project then continue on.

The school or your parents didn't teach you 99% of what's in this book, and so let me and the other authors quoted teach you a few things. I promise you, this book is worth WAY more than the small charge you pay for it.

There is a lot of money to be had in the world, there is no shortage, in fact there's so much so that it creates inflation (that is where there's too much money in society and that forces prices up). Here in 2020 the government is flooding the US with money. Printing and printing. Loaning and loaning. 10 TRILLION recently in Aug. 2020 USA.

The purpose of this book specifically is to show you some workable viewpoints, doingnesses and *what not to do or THINK*, which can make and save you **millions of dollars and years of time** in the workaday world in Real Estate, in Business, Investing and Life.

You possibly could have some false data right now in these arenas, that may need getting rid of. Well to change there needs to be change. You might have to drop some of your preconceived notions/teachings.

SUCH AS,

"I don't have any money.

I can't do that

I'm an introvert

I don't sell things

You can't do that here."

This is not a philosophy lesson but mindset is very important.

Cancel that stuff.

Then you have to have some of the correct/senior data to progress with and be able to press forward three steps and not fall back four. Someone to show you the ropes.

I can be, do and have anything. I believe you can too.

This book is going to show you SOME of this correct/senior data and more!

It's not going to put out every single detail, not in a hundred and twenty three pages.

Life has a lot of pieces, but we will cover some key points, and money, investing and business are a big part of it.

This is the solution for you. Wherever you are in life, the route is going to have steps and these steps have gradients to them, the smaller first steps lead upwards to better conditions and bigger Wins. Some of you out there are missing some basics/fundamentals. Some who are successful even.

I'm starting at a lower gradient for you. I wouldn't say beginner, but beginner to intermediate, (intermediate would be someone who has some experience but not expert or professional).I'm defining terms for you and have included a glossary at the back. Use it.

I am sure an expert could learn something here, but this book is not geared for an expert.

Now before I issued this book here in 2020 I looked at quite a lot of reviews on similar business books, specifically the three-star reviews and one of the complaints was "too general". I hear you. I will be specific with rules, exact recommendations and very specific examples and real life situations of stated principles.

My name is Brett Lemos. I've been working in Real Estate Construction and Contracting for more than 25 years, having a license in California for the past 20 years.

Before that I worked for an LA chimney company, before that for an earthquake retrofitting company in LA.

Construction and buildings is something I know quite a lot about and I have been successful in the Air duct cleaning field for the past 20 years here in Los Angeles California.My company was started by myself and a partner in 1999, he decided he wanted his own company and split off to start his own air duct cleaning company.

Years later he sold me his company and retired, so in a way I got lucky, I benefited from his experience and what he and I built.

I absolutely did what I would call "an apprenticeship" in air duct cleaning under him before I went out on my own.

No high/college schooling taught me what you need to be successful in this business. I learned in the field and from him, an elder with lots of practical experience and guts. It takes guts to make money and have your own business.

Us, together we figured out the technology of air duct cleaning and what works and in this team we were more than "me against the world".

Part of my team now is my wife and four children and all our workers, I am 52 years old and I have a good amount of experience working on, buying, speculating and Investing in real estate and property.

Some of the benefit that you will get by reading this book is experience.

I have a lot more experience than possibly a lot of people reading this and a lot of people that are out in the business world. Another benefit of this book specifically is I'm going to show you exact successful actions that I have used in business, investing and in life to be happy and prosperous which I think most people want.

Just because you're prosperous doesn't mean you're happy, but it sure can help!

Now the proof is in the pudding, meaning you got to taste it and see it and know that it works. It's not "Just believe me and then it works" but you will do these things, put them into regular practice and you'll see they actually do work.

Now that's why I'm only going to recommend actions, investments, and viewpoints that specifically do work for me. Workable.

I am not recommending every single thing I talk about in this book.

I'm not a soloprenuer by trade. I am a business man, who has worked for many large companies and situations and now work mainly for our own company, Airfresh Duct Cleaning.

As you can tell I am a very good communicator, straight forward and knowing. You want to see details and examples related to normal people. Done.

I promise I'm only going to recommend to you benefits that I personally believe in 100% and use 100% myself so that I can as close as possibly guarantee Wins for YOU in business, investing and life.

These things have helped me and helped people I know, and absolutely I believe they take the most risk out of the situation and are the least randomity and most prediction.

Now I want to create a sense of urgency here for you to get to work, to get products completed, to get a mindset more like the right, successful mindset. Not just my mind, but other successful people too quoted in the book here.

And the urgency to get your money working for you as soon as you possibly can. Whether it be a brick and mortar, online business, investing in real estate or investing in a group project with other investors. It's time to get busy.

This is a call to action.

Action will get you where you want to go, giving up things that you don't need in order to change and replace them with new things that you do need.

Some of these chapters could be a whole book in themselves so It's going to be a jam-packed 200+ Pages here to help you!

This is a call to action to become successful. Start!

Brett Christopher Lemos

1

BUSINESS BASICS, DELIVERY

First Thing, is you got to have a product or service people want or need.

These days, most think of "keyword searches" to find this. Before the internet there was surveys. People would survey what was needed from a restaurant owner and what they would be willing to pay for it. That's what we did.

Unwanted items or services are a tough business to start and tougher to continue.

Example: newspapers, pretty scarce these days.
Example: investment books, not scarce.
Example: dial up internet, done.

Once you find something people are willing to pay for and are doing so at a large enough quantity, you want to create a group around it.

I do have vendors/people that work for us and our company and I also sell in the company and there's a technical division that delivers the products, the service, cleaning etc.

I've always been a supporter of, "you give a guy a job and you let him do it, unless he is having diffuculty or he causes trouble, just let him do it".

Have people work for you, who are trained on what you need and stable in their job.

For instance, you probably are not a mechanic so why would you change the oil on your car? It could be fun yes, but you don't have the tools, you don't do it very often and it's just easier to pay a professional to do it, that's his job, let him do it.

The solopreneur who sells an Amazon product still has lots of people working for him, maybe they are in Bangladesh and just out of sight and we don't think of them but there's many of them and they all form a complex stream that all ends up with a needed product being delivered to someone with a smile, and someone helped. Good.

I would like to say working for someone else who's a great successful boss or company, there is nothing wrong with that at all.

You absolutely can become successful and make a lot of money working for someone like that. Now I don't consider myself an entrepreneur, because I don't like to take risks. Starting new unsuccessful actions is risky. Your certainty is not there yet. Working for someone else is a chance to ride some other successful person or companies coattail, and get experience and certainty and stack your cash for purchasing your assets.

I would recommend looking for a person not necessarily a company to work for, because you can see their drive, their success and their leadership directly since you would be working under them. Apprenticeships are great especially when you are getting paid.

For a person who was working under a leader as an employee, an employee who is doing well and making good money to leave and start fresh in some solopreneur thing where they're making half the money but they're working for themselves, I don't necessarily recommend at all and I'm sure you can see how that could be a wrong move.

If you're going to study a business, study a person in it like Warren Buffett, Dale Carnegie, Steve Jobs Etc, not their company.

Okay so in general, my main business is contracting in Air duct cleaning.

I've said this many times and I'll state it again here for your learning benefit.

"the hardest part about this business and many others actually is not doing the jobs, it's getting the jobs."

What does that entail? Sales. Public Relations.

For the more complete study see chapter 7. "Sales in business, in Life "

Sure the technical aspects of the work are large and there are efforts to put out and skills to know, what to do and what not to do, and when!

However, In business and in life with women and men every communication you put out that tries to gain someone's agreements or you're trying to persuade them of something or you trying to get them to do something is basically *"sales".*

Unfortunately, this subject is **NOT** covered well or at all, in colleges or high schools.

POLICY

Policy is defined as "1. is a set of ideas or plans that is used as a basis for making decisions, esp. in politics, economics or business. "

Collins Cobuild for Advanced Learners Dictionary

In Life this can be very important.

If you break the law, that can be looked at as violating policy.

If you live in a rooming house or with roommates, break the House policy and see what happens.

IN BUSINESS:

This can be looked at in a few different ways.

It can be the standard things that are done day to day.

It can be a handling for some Crisis, that is now adopted as policy.

It can be the stable data for a specific job/post written up in a course that is done by new employees.

It can be what to do when certain indicators come up, production is down, or stopped.

Every business should have base POLICY and be making new policies especially when a recession, pandemic occurs etc, but not just when these large easy to see problems are here.

When new projects come up, such as a new building or event, certain Policies would have to be implemented such as, some jobs we work we have to wear certain safety masks and hard hats, some jobs we do not.

Break the policy, don't have a spare hat in your truck and you may not be working that day! (the spare hat is our policy, all workers carry two hats+ two facemasks just in case)

A violator of policy too often will become a liability, and policy helps to point out where things are off or where someone is not doing the job.

When the person becomes a liability, they can be very destructive.

My definition of liability would be "someone or something causing more harm than good ". Shutting this country down almost completely for months because of Covid 19 is unfortunately a liability, it would cause way more harm than good.

Policy can save a business from "newbies" and what they were taught elsewhere from coming in and changing all you've built. It will hold the base form of your organization and keep doing what you were doing before the newbie arrived.

All through this book, I am giving you some of the basic form holding policy we follow, and I have in my life to make it successful and Prosperous!

DISCONNECTING, HOSTILE, ANTAGONISTIC CUSTOMERS.

One policy I keep in at our company is do not stay connected to antagonistic or hostile people/customers.

Example: May 5th 2020 I call one of our past customers we've done work for, last time was Nov 2006, awhile, but we did good work there. I read the file and invoices before calling. We do regularly mail to this customer Jay S.

Customer Jay S. says 'no we don't need gutter work, were are ok and we don't need any of your help", I tell him "ok what we mostly have been doing for the last 14 years is air duct cleaning", he says "he thinks that rips up the ducts in a house" and promptly hangs up.

I call him back he does not answer.

Thankfully he's mistaken and I would like to correct him, but he's now not on our mailing list and removed from our call list. He was hostile, and this was the 2nd instance of that since 2006.

Example: I call a past customer from a job done in 2012 about cleaning the dryer duct again.

I personally had cleaned and repaired it under his house for $220.

He says," the city inspected it and said it was all wrong and what you did was wrong and I had to have it replaced ", "are you still in business".

So I say "I'm sorry, I have no notes about that here, I would've fixed it for free, I do remember your house,it was a tough reconnection"

I continue "Its a long 20 foot duct and I know it still needs to be cleaned, maybe I can do that for you" He says 'no thank you" hangs up.

Thankfully he's mistaken and I would like to correct him, but he's now not on our mailing list and removed from our call list. He was hostile.

I remember that house vividly,it was a major pain in the A**.

I **know** I did it just fine and no City Inspection is needed on projects/work that small.

These people can steal your life, your money and your attention.

We Don't continue to work for them or stay connected.

Qualifier: if the job is $20k etc. and it's a good profit, I am *much more* willing to face emotion and suppression/hostility.

Trust me, this one above can save your life.

One of the main reasons our business continues and I continue to sell jobs in it is because of the quality of our work and what we give.

I know and others working here know that we are doing a good job and have very little corrections or jobs that we have to go back to and fix etc.

WE KNOW we are doing it better and are giving more than we take.

Also another reason to have enough work in your sales pipeline, to where you are not depending on one hostile person/job, Have a lot and waste them.

SUB PRODUCTS

Here is a key idea in business, all businesses.

Sub products : there are many different products that lead to your final sale or conclusion of the project or a great service.

You can look at this like the framing of the house is done. Okay now we're ready for the plumber and electric that's a sub product of a house.Framing. The working plans for the construction, that's a sub product.

In my business here, contracting the cleaning, we have calls out, you have mail out also, if you have bids done those are all sub products and you want to control how those are flowing.

You want to micromanage how those are being done and how much of that's being done because that leads to sales. The calls out, the mail out, the number of presentations that are done.

10 bids/proposals done and sent well you're going to sell a few. One or two bids done now, you may sell nothing. It's a numbers game and these sub-products enable you to keep track of it, of

the things that lead up to your product or your completed job or sale or performance.

Example: clicks on your ad to look at buying it.
Example: Letters, Emails, calls, OUT.
Example: Calls in, emails in for info.
Example: sales meetings done with client, bids sent out. How many write ups of deals done.
Example: Drilling, a new procedure, an old procedure, getting a pass on a drill before the real thing is **Important.**

Some of these subproducts can be a whole job in a company, like someone who just does calls to customers to set appointments or someone who only does mail out or someone who does bids and just goes out and looks at/prices jobs, a salesman that can be a whole job right there for a post(job).

Also these subproducts can easily be staticized (put on a graph) to know when they are up or down and start bypassing (whoevers down) or whatever handling is necessary.

Example: In life a sub-product could be a stable marriage to raise a child in.

Example: the years of practice you put in to a musical instrument to become a pro and give a masterful performance.

DECISION MAKING.

> *"Some decisions you should make yourself and some you should delegate to someone more believable".*
>
> — RAY DALIO, PRINCIPLES: LIFE AND AND WORK.

Now in your company Soloprenuer style this would still apply, as trusting your accountant, lawyer and social media specialist.

In your company with employees and contractors working under you, you sometimes have to make the tough decisions such as who to fire, who to hire. Who gets paid, who doesn't (Covid 19 style furloughs).

I put this Ray Dalio quote up above there as an example of generality on purpose.

There are certain specific areas as the owner where you have to be involved in the decisions and at least have to be info'd on by staff.

1. Legal, Any problems with violations of the law, citations, code of construction, any copyright infringement, suits, penalties or fines.

2. At times of crisis, (such as a Pandemic). Every single money expenditure..
3. Approval of any and all permanent Policy in the organization.
4. Any major changes in ongoing projects especially that are large changes in finance or build, strategy etc.

Primarily, you are the source of your business and probably will be the one to have the license/ certification and all decisions with it, or the property/ lease loan is in your name, you have to make the decisions (or should be doing).

Or the Amazon account is in your name. Or the overall vision of the company and goals, that's YOU!

In my business world someone who is "believable "is PR and sales, but not a generality to be used with decision making. Credible is probably a better word for someone else to make the decision.

And in my life I definitely recommend you make decisions quick, firm and not let " maybe " hang around. Yes or no, that's it.

If you think "maybe I will be successful/a millionaire" etc. You probably won't be.

Sometimes, it has to be reaffirmed/restated, 100's, thousands even tens of thousands of times.

Persistent As F*ck.

That's a big part of creating it.

Like a Marriage, continually created in your mind, your friends minds and others.

> *"Believe nothing just because a so-called wise person said it. Believe nothing just because a belief is generally held. Believe nothing just because it is said in ancient books. Believe nothing just because it is said to be of divine origin. Believe nothing just because someone else believes it. Believe only what you yourself test and judge to be true."*
>
> — BUDDHA - PHILOSOPHER (563 - 483 BC)

To me this Buddha quote means in my life "I see what I see, and I test and judge what is true for me".

This is very important in business and life.

Example: a salesman approaches your company to sell you" lead generation". You know from past test/investigation its crap. You ask what he's selling and he says "he's not selling", he can't own up to selling/does not know what sales is.

Example: a new hire is acting uppity and argumentative about his idea he considers right. (when you want to go a different route).

Example: someone tries to tell you Employee A in the company is causing trouble, lazy. You do your own inspection and interview and find Employee A having trouble with his wife and its stressing him, but he's competent. You work out a handling with him on it.

You see and decide what you see. Period. You see evil, ok. Another may not.

You see and decide what is right for your life, company or relationship.

DRILLING

This is an example in subproducts above but practice of your craft, and drilling can be very very **important**.

In business, some organizations have drilling done on regular basis, like on ships, FIRE drill, (timed of course). Other situations need drilling such as

Sales, (what to do when they say this, what not to do, closing procedure of it etc.)

Customer support (how to handle emotional customer, procedure, communication skills.)

New machines in the shop (how to use it, safety.)

Drilling, Repetition is one facet of learning, doing it correctly under timed pressure is more like the real world. If you can do it perfectly in a drilling situation, **You are very likely to get it right in real world application.**

ONLINE REVIEWS, YELP, ANGIESLIST ETC.

YELP.com is a 1-5 star rating site for businesses.

Yelp is a site for reviews and to refer your business to customers similar to angieslist.com.

Yelp I believe is extortive though,mafiaso even.

Heres my experience,circa 2014 I was considering using a Yelp ad campaign, Tatyana a sales rep. kept contacting me,I finally decided against using it and let her know that, very clearly.

Immediately after this, **5** one star reviews showed up on our Yelp page and the yelp profile was seemingly "hacked" having a new web address "freshbreezeairductcleaning.com" and a new physical address in LA.

I researched Yelp and reported/flagged this as abuse and fraudulent.

I also found 124 reviews of Yelp on Google,almost all the reviews were one star and a recurring theme of extortion, mafia and fraud ran thru the reviews.

A few days later a Yelp HQ person with a San Francisco ph. number contacted me and actually double talked me, and even suggested I just put up a new profile.

Our profile is full of five star reviews and had a few years on it, this HQ person seemed suppressive and the advice was suppressive and contractive.

If you use Yelp, watch the profile and use the "response to review" button to state the truth if needed.

These one star reviews were fraudulent (we did not talk to or work for the 1 star complainers at ALL) and they were probably created by Yelp, no one hacked the site except probably them.

They may have cleaned up their act since then, but what happened, happened.

To this day the only non 5 star review we have up on their site is fraud and we never worked for or talked with the "Customer".

With Angieslist, we have limited use of it, but no real problems to report. It is FREE, but I have seen, if you do not pay for something with them, you will get no calls from them.

I would use them again as a paid referral service.

MINDSET TO SUCCEED

"There are no constraints on the human mind, no walls around the human spirit, no barriers to our progress except those we ourselves erect."

— RONALD REAGAN - 40TH US PRESIDENT - (1911 - 2004)

I believe in you and I KNOW you can do anything you set your mind to be, do and have. With getting rid of some false data you possibly have and replacing it with stuff like what is here, you will succeed. But it starts with you and the change.

I talk about sales in this book here in Chapter 7 and if you're not 100% sold on every single thing you're doing such as your wife, your job, the book you're writing, the church you belong to, musical project that you enter (a band) ; It will show up in the lack of caring, the mistakes, the ineffectiveness, the general not successfulness and lack of passion.

It will show up in some fashion.

Selling yourself on the project first is a super important Mindset datum because if you go in and try to sell it or do it and you're not totally fully sold yourself, look out. It could be bad wreckage.

Well this book definitely has a lot of specifics and the mindset is definitely something that I'm going to put out in a little different way here for you because to get to a successful point you're the first person every morning to start that action and what you have and what you need to be, it all starts with You.

Like the goal writing point 4 in the free "4 Major Basics" in the beginning of the book.

And these are hard won data of 52 years+ of experience/training/study from me to you here now. These viewpoints all through the book have a certain *Mindset*, one of them is;

Workability.

They work, they aren't the best, they aren't the worst, but they work.

The viewpoint, the formula, The goal, the method, the handling.

My business works, it makes a profit and a good product for the environment. The policies I set down in it, work.

I am recommending things here that work for me.

Some of these you might make work for you, such as the stockmarket.

I have studied calls and puts and stocks and I know if I really wanted to I could make money in the Market, but I choose not to.

(calls and puts are different ways to make money with stock even when you don't buy it and the stock is going down in price) Sounds simple. If it was so easy, everyone would do it right ?

PERSISTENT AS F*CK.

Woo. WOO. Excited! I'm going to make it.!

Excellent.

Now try to do it that way, in everything you do for the next month.

Not so easy.

That's the key really, being able to persist thru the BS, the lies, the setbacks, the Covid etc. etc. and not get down and defeated.

It's a moment by moment create for me in my life equaling up to a day,then a week then weeks, OF GETTING IT DONE AND HOLDING MY POSITION.

DO IT AGAIN, DO IT AGAIN, DO IT AGAIN,

FAILURE

Part of the mindset to succeed is how you handle failure.

You are not going to succeed at everything you try on the first time. You're going to need to possibly correct, regroup, restudy, redrill and then Reattack!

And possibly even fail again. I personally have and I know a lot of these people here on Amazon selling these products on investing etc., they have failures too but they continued on, they regrouped and reattacked for sure.

I don't know you or your troubles, but I personally have pushed through a few troubles of my own. To list a few here:

- Drugs. Tons of them, for years.Prescription and illegal.
- Health troubles. Been in the Hospital many times.
- Bankruptcy.
- Foreclosure.
- Eviction.
- Divorce.
- Lost my kids.
- Close Friends dying on me.
- Stolen car.
- "Great stock tip" (lost it all).
- Poor Student (5 years to finish high school).
- At 15 y/o Ousted from my family into a live in Boys school.

To name a few major ones.

I made it through. You can too.

THERE IS ONLY ONE WAY TO FAIL AND THAT'S TO STOP/GIVE UP. IF YOU CONTINUE, YOU HAVE NOT FAILED.

You will make it through it, just what your condition will be on the other side of it, *that's the question.*

That's part of the mindset. I liken it to becoming a cork on the water, you push it under but no matter what, *it just keeps coming back up.*

That's me.

BCL

2

BUSINESS, ADVANCED CONCEPTS

The next area I would like to cover in business is money and,

BANKING

I'm thanking my dad now who always taught me when I was growing up, which I didn't understand at the time, but he said:

> *"Son, never keep your money all in one place."*

So let's look at that idea, well that could be an investment, possibly diversification which a lot of those CFP (Certified

Financial Planner) guys in the stock market use that word "diversification" of your portfolio.

However another good way to look at this is about physically keeping all your money in one spot. Rather than one Bank, use another bank and another bank, or a credit union so that in case of some type of pandemic or Savings and Loan collapse (1989) which has happened, you are not caught with your pants down. Definitley keep some cash at home too.

> *"There is one more possible scenario, your bank is insolvent and invokes "Bail in" policy.*
>
> *Those of you that follow my writing know that I've spoken about "Bail ins" frequently over the last couple of years. This is a policy whereby "troubled banks" have the right to take some of their depositors' money and convert that money to bank stock."*
>
> — JOHNTRUMANWOLFE.COM MARCH 2020 HIS BLOG

Bail in methodology would be invoked in a panic if the Bank collapses when everyone wants their money at once. The bank would take your savings and convert it into bank stocks (equity) and your money would be frozen in the bank.

You would become an "investor" in the bank.

You might want to think about getting a home safe or two and have a fake one with trinkets in it, (to fool thieves).

"How can we have any faith in- or rely on- the banking system in general...or in a crisis ?

— JEFFREY T. MALAYSIA

---

1. There is a difference between the words faith and trust. I have faith the banks are greedy, focused only on self interests. I do not trust the banking system to take care of its clients, crash or no crash."

Robert Kyosaki, Author Fake, Fake money, Fake Teachers, Fake Assets

I really don't trust banks either. Our company and me personally have had a accounts with W Fargo since 1991 and Chase since 1999 and had over ten million dollars go thru just them.

They've never offered one dime of credit to us. All our credit is through other Banks.

FDIC

The Federal Deposit Insurance Corporation, a Federal agency there to insure depositors in the US banks.

NCUA (National Credit Union Administration), is the Fedral agency who regulates and insures credit unions.

I don't know if you know it, but the FDIC rules for banks in America cover you for $250,000 at least, in case of a crash, bank failure. They **may** cover you for more, but it's not guaranteed.

However, the FDIC **has not even 1%** of the money in the US Banking system. This is data for the player when you start getting those big ticket sales/flows.

From a recent article by Simon Black, Financial commentator April 2020

How much money will the banks lose because of this pandemic?

"It could easily end up being hundreds of billions of dollars, even several trillion dollars.

"No one knows. But it's not going to be zero. It's silly to think that banks are immune to the Coronavirus or to assume that not a single bank is going to run into problems.

Don't get me wrong— I'm not saying that the banking system is about to collapse. There are stronger banks and weaker banks. Many of them will survive, others will fail.

"What I am saying is that there are enormous and obvious risks that threaten the banking system.

"As I've written several times over the past few weeks: Anyone who says, 'No, that's impossible,' clearly doesn't have a grasp of what's happening right now. EVERY scenario is on the table, including severe problems in the banking system.

"But the FDIC insists that there's nothing to worry about.

"That's ridiculous. The FDIC only has $109 billion to ensure the entire $13 trillion US banking system. That's less than 1%! "

The Money Sits for you, but not for Them

Another key point here is, *the money does nothing. Especially in a bank.*

Nothing, until you flow it somewhere. It has to be used and preferably to make more progeny (baby benjamins, $100 dollar bills).

Sitting in a savings or MMA account earning .74 percent, (that's not even one percent is not good) or even 1.25% is not good return and is not good for the economy. The days of the "rule of 72" doubling your money at 10% APR bank rates are longgg gone. A lot of you probably never heard of rates like this, they did exist before 2000.

Folks, we are headed for negative interest rates at US banks. SEE these rates below in other countries:

Japan: -0.10%

Sweden: -0.30%

European Central Bank: -0.40%

Denmark: -0.70%

Resource markets.businessinsider.com > news > stocks > negative-in

In those countries you have to pay the bank to have an account. The more money you have, the more you pay. Many people are buying safes for storage at home.

Your money sitting in a bank is working hard for them, just not for you.

For every $1000 the banks get, they lend out $900. Holding 10% is the required "fractional reserve" requirements for the bank. This is known as the "fractional reserve system" and almost all banks use it to print more money (digits).

And you know your banker lends that $900 out, not at the .012 APR you get in his savings account. No way.

He then lends it out at 10-20 or 30% even higher interest. Or they invest in large investments not available to you and me like Big commercial real estate, derivatives and bonds like the Boeing Bonds at 5% in chapter 5 ahead.

Today the main USA Central Bank is the Federal Reserve and you *do not* vote the Chairman of The Fed into office, at least up until now Jun 2020.

It has been a completely separate entity to the US Govt since 1913 when it was formed.

This can be a book in itself with all the "shadow banking' and money being influxed into the US economy right now.

"Shadow banking" is partly the behind the scenes big moves on Wall street etc using MBS and other three letter financial derivatives.

"Alot of these moves are to other US allied countries in the form of loans from The FED called "Swap lines"."From Marin Katusa Rich Dad Radio Program July 15 2020

These are Billions Big Loans.

There is also the trillion dollar secret/confidential Pension moves, you never hear about.

On Central Banks, to quote Robert Kyosaki from *"Who Stole my Pension"* Jan 2020

> "...so much controversy around Central banks. It's because Central Banks control a nation's money supply and determine the quantity of money in
>
> circulation by buying and selling debt. Hence they have more power than governments and the People."

Takeaway, don't keep your big money all in one place or all in one currency and use the money, don't let it sit there. Get it to work for you, ASAP!

LLC OR CORPORATION?

Next lets take up Advanced business ideas like forming an LLC or a Corporation or getting workers compensation insurance for your company or for yourself.

Now specifically the entities like S Corp are going to start to benefit you I believe when you're making more than $50k net a year. In lawsuits the corporation/LLC can protect you by taking the brunt of the hit of the suit and protect your personal holdings being excluded in America.

Some US states, like California, charge more fees for maintaining an LLC.

In the state of Delaware, LLC fees are $300.00 yearly and if I were to start one, I would use that state probably.

Unlike an S Corp, a business operating as an LLC may have all income be subject to payroll or self-employment taxes. Not Good.

Your tax advisor accountant can advise on which is right for you and set it up for you.

Our company Airfresh operates with a California S corporation. Yearly Fees are a minimum $1k and then pro rated to your income levels. Another requirment that comes with a Corporation and not with LLC is the annual board minutes have to be filed with the state every year,not a big deal,your accountant can handle it usually or there are companies who do it for a small fee. You can do it yourself like larger companies do.

I do not reccommend California for Corporation filing. I would look into other states. The State Govt. here is in the red (in a deficit) and other states could be more beneficial.

The corporation idea should be **NOT** be underestimated, it has a few benefits that the rich use that I would like to mention.

It changes *the flow* of your monies. Employees working for a corporation will **earn the money, pay taxes, spend**.

The rich/business owner with a corporation, **will earn, spend, then pay taxes.**

What this does is allows things to be counted as corporate expenses and take other tax advantages that allow you to KEEP MORE MONEY. It also allows you to pay yourself first, rather than the govt. That is very important.

CORPORATE SPENDING:

Such as a vacation/Meeting In Cabo San Lucas.

Payments, insurance, repairs to a corporate vehicle.

Parties, Meals that are meetings. (partial)

All paid with pretax income. The corporation/LLC is essential also to protect your assets AND your fortune when you start accumulating them.

See your Tax professional for your individual situation.

WORKERS COMPENSATION

Workers comp is something that comes into play in construction and protecting ALL the workers of the business. For Any type of administration employees, the pricing is going to be very low : per $100 paid to the employee, rates like $1 or something similar for an office worker.

Usually Workers comp rates are charged per every $100 you pay the employee, so if they make $500 per week and the rate is

$1.50; you as the employer must pay $7.50 to the workers comp. insurance carrier for that week for that employee.

When you get into actual technical employees like a plumber, roofer, air conditioning Technician, Air duct cleaning Technician, that's where you're going to get into higher rates where it's about $23 per hundred that you pay the worker, which can add up quick.

Currently here in year 2020 the minimum to have a Workers Comp policy in California is about $2700 annually. You can get a policy which just covers yourself only for under 1k annually, I believe.

When you're Contracting, this policy is needed to get any jobs of substantial value, period. All of the property management companies and owners of multifamily buildings here in Los Angeles that we work for require you to have a workers comp Policy.

If you are a Contractor and you hire someone on a 1099 independent contractor basis, almost always they are responsible for their own Workers Comp coverage. See your tax man on this, especially in California, they are changing this policy monthly.

THE TAX MAN/WOMAN

Another Advanced business policy for you to use is an accountant. The people who have their wife as the bookkeeper and refuse to let a Pro do it, are just thinking too small. Unless your wife is an Enrolled Agent with the IRS, I would look at hiring an accountant.

These guys/gals can save your butt and your money! The more money you start to make, the better accountants you're going to want and need.

Yes I went through a few accountants over the years and they're not all created equal, generally the more money you pay them, the more experience and aggressiveness you're going to encounter with that accountant.

If you ever get audited by the IRS etc. I highly recommend going in to the audit with your accountant if you can.

There are other types of audits, such as Workers comp and FTB (franchise tax board). FTB here in CA handles all corporate payments.

Generally I would recommend any person with a business doing over 100k gross to have an accountant especially if you have a corporation or LLC.

Corporations require their own State tax filing "1120 "form and unless you are an accountant, you should let them handle it and "let them do their job".

You will still be filing a personal 1040 as you usually have along with the corporations filing also. Double The FUN!

In real estate investing and property ownership you get to file a schedule K1 for property covering depreciation and other flows, which can be huge for your taxes.

And to reiterate, real estate is the only investment where if done big enough, you can get to 0% taxes and be making wealth. This is done mostly through depreciation and showing losses on your return.

BTW, DR. Jerry Buss, a PHD in Chemistry, who started the LA Laker franchise greatness in the 1980s, made his original fortune with real estate in Mariani-Buss Associates.

For me wealth is the guy who owns the Lakers and signs the checks, rich is the players on the team. Big Difference.

BUSINESS LOANS, LINES OF CREDIT

Our company gets calls for these "business loans/capital "from these private companies, (not the mainstream banks) almost daily.

Very annoying, Almost daily. They are loans generally you don't want anything to do with, with interest rates of 50% and higher. I do not recommend these loans at all. Someone you know or your bank is going to give a better deal almost guaranteed, plus you know the local banker somewhat which can be very helpful and these calls, well they could be criminals.

TAKEAWAY FROM THE CHAPTER:

Get your money moving into income producing assets and do not keep it all in one bank.

Use The advanced concepts as GOALS to reach in your business.

Move to higher ground and new problems.

BCL

3

REAL ESTATE, YOUR HOME AND OTHERS.

You probably would like to own property and your own home, if you don't own one/some already. It is the American Dream. I had the same dream, and still do, just bigger now.

When I was younger in the 90's and just starting out as a single guy, I personally did a real estate course before I started investing in it, and boy was this course a rip-off.

Totally lost my money. It was just showing you some very scammy, deceptive type of ideas like where you're going to get the person who does want to sell a property, to turn over control of a property with no money down to them and actually sell it to someone who does have money with you not giving the seller any/very little money using some technically verbose contract which kept mentioning "ballon payment ". It did not look technically ethical and it looked very deceptive. But I kept looking, reading, and seeing properties.

Before I actually bought a house I read Robert Kyosakis' book on money.

My favorite quote from that book regarding single family residence, (notice how I did NOT say multi-family)

"you make your money on the purchase, not the sale"

— AUTHOR ROBERT KYOSAKI, RICH DAD, POOR DAD.

Example: you buy a house for 250k and the Zillow.com estimate is at 310k. Built in equity on the sale.
Example: you buy a house that needs work for $92k that Zillow says is worth $105k and you arrange to get 25k cash back on the close. You fix it up, get an appraisal at 130k. Flip it for 132k.

After reading this above book, I thought this was the way to go and got really excited about owning property.

Then I asked a personal mentor of mine Mitch who owned property for decades, I asked "did buying a house help you achieve your Life goals "?

He said yes, absolutley. I was sold.

I started looking at more and more houses and saving my money and then I met my wife in 2004, who had already owned several properties here in Los Angeles.

For most people this will be their first entrance into real estate, owning their own home. This can be a lot of work, or not so much depending on how old and used the property is.

Condominiums are good too, having less work usually than SFR, some condo situations have fees where the outside areas and other things like elevators are all taken care of for you. These fees can Be $200+ per month.

I personally have owned 3 homes now, 4 when I married my wife she had one already. Unfortunately in 2008 we lost one to foreclosure. Three main things contributed to us losing that house.

Firstly, we bought it in 2004 right near the price height of the market. Not the right market. Second the 2008 housing bubble broke. Three, the loan we got was not good, I will explain more thouroughly.

Now let me go over the 2008 Housing bubble that happened then. I'm writing this is in April 2020 (middle of Coronavirus).

In 2008, millions of US people in America lost their homes just like we did. The main reason that we lost our house was specifically at that time there was some violations going on where the

Glass-Steagall Act was repealed in 1999 and what this caused was a shift in banking where housing loans were able to be gotten for no money down, no credit check, very little to no type of collateral. Improper housing loans. Subprime loans gone wild.

I will cover this 2008 collapse fully later in Ch 9.

(Prime is a term in the financial world meaning the loanee is high quality, qualified, A plus rating)

Many of the 2008 foreclosed loans were ARM (adjustable rate mortgage) loans. Adjustable-rate mortgages where the rate would usually (at that time, not always) change to a much higher rate at a later date and that's what happened to us.

About two years into the loan if you didn't refinance it and get a better loan you were stuck with that ARM rate. We didn't know this, and the monthly payment suddenly jumped up 1k, Gulp. We were ignorant on the loan terms and the payment went up way too high and we ended up losing that house and ended up having to move out and rent. Not so bad.

Which there's nothing wrong with renting at all, in fact for younger people I would recommend that and unless you're buying a house that's a great deal AND has good equity already in the deal, I would recommend renting and leasing and save your money for the right deal.

THE MARKET

Huge to buying property is, *what is the market currently when you buy/sell?*

In 2008 before the bubble burst at the height of property values, there was a major shift in how home loans were done. As a result many not "qualified "subprime people got into properties and they bought in a sellers market. Not a buyers market. And for that matter a lot of qualified people got into loans, but with no money down and buying in the wrong market, then getting an ARM loan that went way up later. That's what happened to us buying in 2004.

2007, Foreclosures happened, the sheriffing started (sheriffing is where the sheriff comes to evict people from property) and the next four years after 2008, the " bank/agency owned properties" aka "REO" were abundant and the market became more of a buyers market, all the way to about 2013. REO usually happens after a foreclosure auction does not get a sale.

Now the house that we live in now, we purchased in 2012 and it was a good deal, it was a proper move and we did end up making money on the purchase and it had rental spaces in the back (two of them) which means a little bit of income to offset the mortgage. More of an asset.

Also the market at that time of purchase was still good from the 2008 hangover, good selection to choose from. Unlike Los Angeles today, April 2020.

The current loan we got was not an ARM loan (adjustable rate mortgage) and the rate we got was very good and fixed for 30 years. I still would not recommend to you or others especially if you're younger to buy a house especially in the market like now April 2020 and especially if it doesn't have rental possibilities with many doors to rent, like apartments.

LEVERAGE

Lets go over the terms Leverage and "over-Leveraged" in real estate.

These are very important. Leverage in real estate is using borrowed money to buy a property.

"only when the tide goes out do you discover who's been swimming naked"

— WARREN BUFFET, BILLIONAIRE CEO, BERKSHIRE HATHAWAY

Now, many of you may have read this quote from money.com or quora.com etc. and seen a very verbose explanation of it.

To me it means when the market or value is up, the property/investor looks ok, things look good, ,when the market/value is down you see their privates.

Part of this down market or value would be over leveraged owners on the verge of foreclosure/selling property before they want to etc.

Over-leverage in personal finance is a possibility also, when a crisis hits and they're too deep in debt; the income slows or stops and payments still have to be made. They might be a little under dressed.

In real estate "Over-leverage", would be too much debt on the property.

75% debt to 25% cash ratio is acceptable. Anything less than 25% cash in the deal,could be trouble in worst case scenario. Over-leveraged properties are often the ones to be lost to the bank (foreclosure).

A lot of people think that their house is an asset which it could be, but mostly they are liabilities.

Example: You have a renter but the income from him is only 3k a year and your expenses on the house are 6k for the year. Liability.

Example: buying a house at the top of the market with very little cash in the deal.

Example: an over-leveraged house or No money down.

Example: Property needs roof repairs, has termites, needs toilets, bad piping, bad foundation, not known about when purchased. (or known about, still not good). After close final tally on repairs ends up being 25k instead of ten you planned on and you're over leveraged.

Especially an older house that needs lots of attention and has no cash flow or income stream possibilities. Real estate that does have large income streams, cash flow and is considered an asset is multi-family, commercial with tenants, storage buildings etc.

FHA 3.5% Down loan

The Federal Housing Authority, who is under US HUD (US Department of Housing and Urban Development) is a usual way to get financing.

This is the easiest way to get a loan for most first-time home buyers, there are certain restrictions on this loan though.

FICO® score at least 580 = 3.5% down payment.

FICO® score between 500 and 579 = 10% down payment.

MIP (Mortgage Insurance Premium) is required.

> *Debt-to-Income Ratio < 43%. Monthly debt cannot exceed 43% of total monthly income.*
>
> *The home must be the borrower's primary residence.*
>
> *Borrower must have steady income and proof of employment.*
>
> — FROM FHA.COM

There are other Restrictions, FHA Loans can only be used on 1 to 4 unit properties.

If the property requires major renovations it may not qualify unless you apply for the 203k loan, which can get up to 35k for renovations. Minimum FICO score for 203k loan is 640.

Anyone can qualify for FHA loan, they do not have to be a first time home buyer.

All FHA loans require the PMI or MPI insurance, I have heard it called both. You can Refinance later and get this taken off with a new loan. This is insurance from the FHA to the lender. The FHA is not a lender.

You do have to live in the property for the majority of at least the first year.

If you tell the loan officer you intend on living there and don't, its mortgage fraud, a felony. You have 60 days to move in after closing.

The max. allowable FHA loan in 2020 is 765k.

FHA.gov is the official site, I found it very non-useful.

MULTI-FAMILY

These type of Investments hold up and are **REAL** and some, very Recession Proof. You will have cash flow and appreciate, if you know what you're doing and you buy a proper building in the proper area.

Single family homes can be an investment and they can make money with flipping, renting, and if you do it at a large enough scale (enough homes) you can become rich. Unfortunately it is small, **a lot** of work and much more risk compared to the profits to be made in other larger real estate assets.

In investing, I am looking for passive income, not more earned income.

I personally do not want to work in the field of real estate and believe me, it can be a lot of work (earned income).

To clarify, Passive income would be that income you earn from rental properties or bond or stock dividends, royalties.

Earned income is where you work for the money at hourly rates, contracts or salaried income. You exchange your time for money.

To Quote Real Estate Mogul, Grant Cardone,

"until your passive income exceeds your earned income, You will always be a slave."

If you're going to own and rent the single family residence it can be very dangerous if you don't have a lot of backup capital to handle when the renters move out or for repairs etc.

Own a four-plex and live in one unit, then have two renters move out, you are now 50% vacant. Way too high vacancy, unless you don't have a mortgage it could be trouble.

I have the same Viewpoint with duplexes and even 8- 10 units, it's just not enough to cover when a few people move out or the pandemic happens, recession etc. and suddenly, "I can't pay you" and the city releases regulations to stop all eviction and 30 day notices. This is the scene Aug. 2020 Los Angeles.

You need to get up to like 30+ units to where you know you can be able to handle the vacancies or whatever happens. At this point the property would need a manager and this is good because you won't have to manage it personally and you're making enough money to pay the manager also at that size of a building usually.

16 units is a good minimum, but at that rate you will not be able to pay a manager very easily and have profit worth doing it for usually.

If you have to be the manager it's not really, **Passive** income. But some people are ok with that.

MINDSET: THINK BIG! YOU HAVE TO, TO LIVE WELL.

Now my company, Airfresh Cleaning here in Los Angeles, services many of these big multi-family apartment buildings.

We do Air duct cleaning in the specific apartment units or common areas.

We clean dryer duct exhaust for the lint that builds up in the ducts (fire hazard). We also clean grease exhaust above the kitchen stove and we do trash chute cleaning, a lot of these big buildings have multiple trash chutes (they get very nasty).

So I have worked with Owners of these buildings and have confronted many of these big multi-family buildings and always thought, "boy I would love to own one or get involved investing in one".

But how ?

I personally invest my money in multi-family large-scale apartment unit buildings ; piggybacking on other investors who already own the property and they give us a piece of it to OWN.

This is a very safe way to get monthly cash flow on the rent, to get your full investment back on a refinance of the loan, and continued cash flow after the refinance.

On a sale, a piece of the equity also, depending on the percentage you invest in the Fund. (see glossary)

These types of large investment structure "funds" if you will, are not easy to find. I looked for more than 20 years. The little guy is kept out of them on purpose by Wall street, Big insurance, Banks etc.

I'm going to go over the terms "accredited investor" and "non-accredited" investor. Non-accredited would be they are making less than $200,000 a year and do not have a net worth over a million dollars.

An accredited investor is making over $200,000 a year and can show a net worth of a million dollars or more. Normally the minimum investment for an accredited investor on apartment funds like this would be $100k.

And with Schedule K1 depreciation, every dollar of that passive income we get a month is not taxed. Total passive income. (see glossary for K1)

The above piggyback type of investment fund would be called "syndicating" by many, but that is a mistake. It is "profit-sharing "or "partner".In my opinion THIS is the best model. Another name not commonly used for it is "recapitalization".

Real estate "Syndicators" usually lead a group of investors, pooling all the funds to make a bigger purchase that individually you could not. I don't invest my money in these types deals.

Syndicated deals can have 5,6- 10 partners even and when times are tough, 5 might need cash and want to sell, the other 5 might know/want to stay in and ride the storm out. It could get unstable and even unfriendly. Not good.

BTW A REIT (see glossary) does **not** have you as a partner.

In a generalization of property classes, "the core four" are A being the best and D being the most difficult tenants, area, building etc. For Investment, Absolutely the best types of buildings I've seen would be Class B and Class A renting from $1,000 to about $1,500 per month, no high-end apartments and no Section 8 housing for sure.

TAX SALES

This is the hidden gem for you to find in property investing, it can take some work, but I have a friend who buys land this way and he does well at it. I will go over the basics of it. I personally have not done this yet.

Why are there Tax Sales on properties ?

The owner did not pay the land/school taxes on it. The State, City or County wants to recoup their lost tax revenue so they, after a certain delinquency time period, sell the land or the lien on it.

The reasons for the failure to pay can be many, financial hardships, owner thinks its worthless, the structures on it not worth fixing or sellable, or its landlocked and you cannot get to it.

The seizure happens and now, what does the Municipality do with it ?

What you can do is get a list of properties from the Assesor/Tax collection office, they will know of the next tax sale/auction also. Usually the auction price will start at the amount of tax owed. There can be properties they have been unable to sell at auctions that you could make an offer on to the County/State Tax Assessors office, where you could get a bargain.

These Assessors are apt to accept offers on property that has been off the tax roll for years, to now get it back on the Tax roll.

Example: you make a 5k offer on a property that is located on a hill with no access road, the value of the property is over 100k with a road and the owed tax is over 30k.
Example: you win at auction a large 40 acre piece of land and

know before you go to auction that the property can be split/subdivided into other parcels and sold individually. Example: you get a deal on wet/marshy land that can be filled with dirt for Free or cheaply to make dry level land.

Its not as simple as I'm making it sound or everyone would do it, right.?

What you are purchasing is the Property, Deed, a Lien or a Tax certificate. It differs from area to area. In your area sales are handled differently than my area.

The Tax Assessor will know, and they usually can provide a tax map for you to check the property out beforehand, to see if its swamps or marsh, or has no road in, etc. There may be Gold in Them Thar Hills!

Using a drone to check out landlocks is a possibility. With landlocked property, If a neighbor can be contacted, you could work a $/land swap for a small road strip through to make the landlocked property valuable. Get this in writing from the neighbor of course. Possibly the neighbor may want to buy a parcel of the land and do the road!

My friend doing these Land deals starts with a Letter to the Tax delinquent land owners with an offer. After that it moves onto going to the Assesors and auctions.

When you pay off the taxes owed as an Investor some states give you a Tax Certificate. Some states give you an actual Deed.

Some states give you a Quit-claim Deed. This is a deed where the owner has a certain time to pay back the owed taxes and get the property back. (Usually the investor would get his money back with interest if this happened).

If you get a Tax Certficate/Lien the owner has a certain time period to bring the taxes up to date and reclaim it, again the investor would probably get his money back with interest.

There is a "first come first served policy" in some states like Oklahoma for tax sales, instead of auctioning to the high bidder.

Some of the return rates are good on these liens/certificates, Arizona can be 15%,meaning the owner paid the back taxes and you were remimbursed the tax money paid plus 15%. Wyoming is 15% also with a guaranteed 3% penalty return. Time periods can determine different rates paid. It varies from State to State.

Tax liens do come to foreclosure when your lien is never made good/redeemed by the owner/title holder of the property. But this foreclosure auction has only one bidder, the lien holder.

You should do a title search on any property you are planning on purchasing to look for other liens.

Another important point is "redemption period", this is the time it takes from when you win it, or purchase the lien to the time you get the Title actually,it can be 60 days or as much as 5 years. And in all that time you are expected to keep the taxes current.

But you should be getting paid interest too, it could be worth it at 15%.

PROPERTY VALUE

This is very important when you go to sell or refinance the property. The neighborhood sales that are "comparable sales" in your zip code affect the value of your property. Also the income on the property highly affects the value, if you have a commercial property and tenants. I have seen SFR rental income rejected as income from banks when the owner lives there also. But if the tenant has their own separate address and separate structure this can improve the odds of the bank allowing the income on a loan application.

The market will fluctuate as the amount of properties/product is available also, lots of houses for sale going at lower prices, values down. With very little sales recently and little product on market, values will be up usually.

COMMERCIAL REAL ESTATE

From Real Estate Guru Grant Cardone, The difference between stocks and Real Estate at cardonecapital.com

> "One of the key differences between single-family and multifamily properties is how they are valued.
>
> No matter what the income is on a single-family home, they are almost always valued based on comparable sales of other homes in the area. Rental income normally doesn't play much of a role in the value of a single-family rental.
>
> The value of any multifamily property is almost entirely based on the cash flow. The market will determine an expected rate of return on a multifamily property, which will determine that property's value."

During this pandemic (Covid-19) as I write this, business/office commercial real estate and non-essential business' are taking a whipping value wise. Some businesses will not make it due to the governmental close downs.

Anything using discretionary income like sports, entertainment, travel etc. is on the downturn.

1031 Exchange

If you want to learn how to buy your own properties from scratch and manage them and build up using your 1031 exchange, that's a good idea.

1031X is a tax vehicle where you are selling a property and deferring the capital gains/profits tax by buying a more expensive property with the money, enabling you to scale/expand.

Once a property is sold, you have 45 days to pick a new investment property of the proper scale (like kind and same or larger values). The money from this closing goes into a 3rd party "Accomadator" account. The new property must close within 120 days of first sale.

Close and you successfully transferred 100% of your profit from first deal to another investment. With Accomodators such as apex1031.com or e1031xchange.com, you will be charged a fee for the accommodation, approximately $500 or more.

As a result you go from a 12 unit to a 32 unit building or 150 unit to 250 unit building, it could take a while and be a lot of due diligence, but can be super rewarding and just as successful as piggybacking on others large deals.

The Number of Doors

> *"The most important number in investing in Multi-family, the number of units"*
>
> — FROM REAL ESTATE MOGUL, GRANT CARDONE

> "(On your commercial loan) from Fannie/Freddie, **more important** than your cash in the deal, your credit, and the actual asset you are buying is, **your management experience** ".
>
> — ALSO FROM GRANT CARDONE ON MAY 2 2020 YOUTUBE

The bigger the amount of units the more chance you have to weather any storm, Recession/depression, Pandemic etc. What I have seen though is that until you own some larger complexes that are up near 50-100 units and shown that you can manage them successfully, you won't even be considered to be a player in purchasing buildings that are 200 units and up. As above stated, cash and credit score is not a big matter in these dealings.

That being said, having an avenue to invest in Large buildings like 250 units+ with an experienced real estate investor "partner" is a successful way to make money in multifamily, big multifamily, without the risk and your time spent.

Passive income

Btw, Passive income is taxed at rates from 0-37%. Employee Earned income is taxed around 33% plus.

The bottom line with Taxes and investing is, Real estate in corporations is the only one where you can get to a point where you are paying the least taxes (10% to Zero % rates). I'm not quite there, but people like Donald Trump and Warren Buffet are.

Stocks, bonds, ETF etc,you will get taxed for sure. Even Big Business owners still pay some taxes also, but near 20%.

See your tax professional for exact numbers for your situation.

Where are deals like this?

Probably some of you right now are wondering "where could I invest in what he's talking about "?

There is a United States company I recommend and I will tell you. It is Cardonecapital.com for the accredited investor and has had non-accredited investment available.

Deals

Well currently June 2020 USA, in our state of economic affairs, the amount of unemployed is at about 40 million, some of these 40 million people own houses, duplexes and 4 units. Some of them bought at too high a price. Some have tenants that are part of the 40 million. Some will save the property with "loan modification". (radio commercials are starting now on that)

They are in trouble now possibly and are going to need to do a short sale or refinance or possibly lose the property to foreclosure. Short sale is where the property is sold for less than the debt owed by seller, not an ideal sale and bad for your credit for sure. The bank would have to OK the ShortSale.

But, this will be some opportunity for you and other real estate investors to get in on the low part of the price cycle that's coming. The first properties to go will be these SFR and duplexes, tris and fourplexes. In about 6 months (Dec. 2020) the whole real estate world will look different and the amount of RE product out there to look at will be 4-8x what it is now. That's good for you as the buyer.

It's your real chance to own real estate.

CREDIT

A word on credit, if you want to own property, you will need to use credit. Unless you want pay full 100% cash for every property. I am a not a Dave Ramsey supporter of "get out of debt" "all debt is bad debt".

I am trying to get into more property debt. Especially multi-family 25% down debt I am interested in. Basically you can take 100k and leverage it into a 400k income producing apartment building.

APPRECIATION

When you get an older property and it needs some work, that's ok because then your property will appreciate or rise in value. I always think with this right before you are going to have it inspected for a new loan (refinance).

"6 out 10 houses are sold on curb appeal alone"

— DEAN GRAZIOSI, THINK A LITTLE DIFFERENT

Sales again. You are trying to sell it to a buyer, or an inspector same thing, the inspector is evaluating your property to sell a number to the bank.

You can force the appreciation by doing work on it. Especially the front of the house, this is the first impression you get when seeing it.

Things like

- Adding rain gutters to the house. Cleaning them and roof if needed.

- Placing a nice shade tree in front of house (for value, Palm trees work well in Florida).
- Painting the house or just the front.
- Paint the porch floor.
- Get a new front door or fix it, paint it.
- Get ratty window screens replaced or fixed.
- Wash the windows.
- Cleaning the front walkway and driveway stains (pressure wash usually).
- Clean the siding and cobwebs off the eaves.
- Have the yard and bushes trimmed and looking good. Get rid of any dying vegetation.
- Any front fencing that is rusted, paint it or it has missing boards, replace them.

Most of these ideas above are on the fairly cheaper side of things and not major construction. Make it look fresh and new. New bright flowers planted also are good idea.

YOUR REALTOR

This is a person who is going to help you. Unless you are a licensed realtor, I suggest you use one. Many realtors are also mortgage loan brokers, this is very important if you want to have property. This person should be someone you can identify with somewhat and speaks your language.

This can be a lifelong contact possibly for you, to be part of your realty team.

When you go to refinance a property and it's the same person helping you, it really helps speed things along.

I would not recommend Purple Bricks(bankrupt in 2019) or Savvylane.com, any service that does this for you without a human realtor there in usual fashions. For sale by owner, also not recommending you to do this.

The realtor can sell your house easier if they are there, not on a website or call.

Open houses are a usual route to use to buy, inspect and sell property.

This is what I have done, use a realtor for both loan and the purchase.

If you are looking for commercial properties, certain companies usually handle these in each city, Coldwell Banker or CBA or Charles Dunn here in Los Angeles and not all realtors deal in commercial, it is a minority I would say.

Use the realtor. If they handle your loan also, even better. Refi. is even easier for them if they sold you the house and are mortgage brokers also.

One secret of Real Estate, The Refinance, this is where you can get cash out of your equity,

IN A NON-TAXABLE EVENT. That's worth repeating, you do not get taxed on the money you get out on your refinance of the property. Check with your US Accountant, he will tell you the same thing.

THE WRONG TENANT

If you find a good deal on a house, triplex etc and decide to have renters, there is a few things to consider about the renters.

Screen every potential renter. Credit and national felonies.

> *"In California and many other states, the law prohibits landlords from denying an apartment to someone who is listed on the online **sex offender** database."*

RESOURCE Feb 18, 2008 https://ohmyapt.apartmentratings.com/when_a_registered_sex_offender_lives_near_you.html

This can be a serious problem if you live in a state that does allow this sex offender denying and then one slips in to your property.

Example: they moved from another state and you checked the current state registry, not national registry. They slip in.

Other renters can be up in arms, asking for justice from you. You might have to pay to move the new tenant out, it can be that severe.

Screen every potential renter. Credit and national felonies.

TRUST BUT VERIFY.

When moving in, If possible, I would have the tenant sign some type of waiver regarding mold, and bed bugs also. These can be a pain in the b*tt if you are not covered by it.

The bed bug is very common in California, not so much in the midwest cold areas of the US. They are parasitic and live off the blood, they can bite and then create rashes. They hide in cracks and crevices and a new tenant can easily bring them into your new, fresh space. They are visible to human eyes, being at adult stage they are as big as an apple seed, about a 1/4 inch.

The Mold waiver is needed, especially if you have central AC.

Airfresh Duct Cleaning to the rescue.

We have done many a job in multi-family buildings with serious mold in the AC systems. It can be very unhealthy and the owners of the properties might have you sign a waiver when moving in to their apartment. They probably will not rent to you unless you sign it also.

LIENS ON THE PROPERTY

On a real estate transaction there can be snags, one is liens. These can be discovered on the property when the title is checked and they can be such things as back taxes, mechanics liens, IRS liens.

They would usually need to get paid in the transaction somehow where its agreeable to you and the seller. The Seller could quite possibly not know about this lien, it could be news to him also.

Example: On a SFR you've agreed on the price and are in Escrow, but the mechanics lien for 6k is discovered before closing. You arrange with seller to have the lien paid in the sale but price lowered 6k or you could split it 3k each.

If you work on property and do not get paid timely or as agreed, you can put a mechanics lien on the property if done in due fashion(there is a limit usually as to how long after the work was done to lien). Our company Airfresh has done Mechanic liens on properties, with a legal fee for less than a hundred dollars each.

RENT CONTROL

This is going to come up on you if you want to own a building and rent out units/apartments to tenants.

Rent control is city or state based rates that control how much you can increase the rent annually usually on your tenant. Previously Here in Los Angeles it was 3% per year.

But as of Jan 2020 The Tenant Protection Act of 2019 (AB 1482) a new law created allows the owner to only raise rent 5% + an Annual **increase** in inflation or 10%, whichever is lower. Some housing does not follow this rule though.

Which means, monthly rent is $800.00 you can raise the rent $80 per month maximum annually. Check you local area for this, it differs from county to county.

"We buy your house for Cash"

And then there's the "Cash for your House" route/course, where you go around and post illegal signs in the neighborhood and get a piece of the sale when you refer the seller to a corporate investor/flipper. Who actually has the cash. They put on real estate seminars and the ones with no money get offered this as a source of getting into real estate.

I don't recommend you doing this at all, first its taking the **neighborhood value** down by selling houses at rock bottom/too low prices (usually) and exploiting tough situations like recession or pandemic. And it uglifies the neighborhood and is illegal to post signs on wood poles in my city, for sure.

It also steers people with a house, their attention to something they probably should not be doing, LOSING MONEY, CONTRACTING.

Your attention is VERY important and I cannot state this with enough emphasis.

If you enter this "buy your house for cash" game, it is small, its thinking small and the return is too small to really make the money you need and want in Real Estate to be a player.

Doing anything illegal opens yourself, your group and family up to attack.

Do not do anything Illegal.

Takeaway from the chapter: if done right, Real Estate is solid investing

and you too can do it and it can be very rewarding.

Now is the time.

BCL

4

STOCKS, 401K, ETFS, BONDS, REITS AND GOLD AND SILVER.

...if you ask a stockbroker or investment planner what should I invest in, its like asking a cannibal, whats for dinner?"

— AUTHOR ROBERT KYOSAKI FROM HIS RICH DAD.

WHY IS THAT ?

Sales. (see ch 7.)

A cannibal is going to sell or promote eating meat, the human kind.

Absolutely, a broker or (CFP) Certified Financial Planner is trying sell you something.

Broker means to "negotiate or arrange some type of agreement." Collins Cobuild Advanced Learners Dict.

Brokers get paid commissions or transaction fees, most make money whether you do or not. You lose, they still win somehow. In actual fact the company owns the fund you invest in, not you. Unless you control 51% of the available stock, then you would have a controlling share.

As legendary John Bogle founder of Vanguard funds said

> "(Investors) put up 100% of the cash, take 100% of the risk and get 33% of the return."

Actually its worse than that. The owner of the fund gets about 80% of the return and if the fund crashes, the investor loses 100% of his money, according to Kyosakis, Book Fake, Fake money, fake Teachers, Fake assets.

The CFP (certified financial planner) takes his month long course to be authorized to then sell you insurance, WFG

(World financial group), or some paper asset such as stocks, bonds and ETFs.

While these are assets that produce income and are great for the average person and very affordable for beginners, to me these type of "assets" are not really assets. They have tons of fees and are risky, like a casino.

They are derivatives of something else that is more real, like gold or real estate or you having a business.

To me, they are paper and they need to give you regular income to be a high quality asset.

I do not consider every 3 months regular enough.

I would not consider my house an asset unless it had cashflow (income) and regularly. **Many** people think the other way around.

STOCKS

Now the stocks first of all, I LOST all the money I ever invested in them, so I would not begin to tell you what stock is good or how to invest in them properly.

Some people make a lot of money with these, so far not me.

But I will say they are a good starting point and there are certain stocks that are way less risky than others such as the blue chip ones below.

These are most peoples first and most affordable "asset".

While I do not invest money in the stock market anymore, my dad does in his 401 k and he has $30,000 worth of AT&T bought decades ago. These are blue chip stocks (large fairly safe investment stocks, but still profitable) like Apple, Amazon, Intel etc.

All the money I ever tried to invest in stocks I lost. Penny stocks, larger stocks.

In this book here I'm recommending that if you use stocks to make money on, *only invest what you can completely afford to lose.*

Especially the way the stock market is manipulated with pandemics or recessions or whatever. The pandemic created a huge artificial crash here in March 2020.

Another Thing I personally do not like at all, is investing money in something I don't know about, like mutual funds, where you can be in Big Pharma and not even know it.

Or some other undesirable product like marijuana. I do not want my money in Big Pharma or marijuana.

Bonds are a similar but different story. More on that soon.

401K PLAN

The 401 K is an invention to replace the Defined Benefit pension, that is slowly being phased out of existence. DB is like what the USPS mail man gets or the LA city worker. (See Ch. 11 Pensions.)

A 401 K is a Defined Contribution plan created in the '70s after the 1974 ERISA (Employee Retirement Income Service Act).

ERISA made it mandatory for all private corporate Pensions to have an annual audit.

This audit is VERY important because this can catch errors, fraud, mismanagement etc. *Though only about 40% of private Pensions actually get audited.*

There is a lot behind that last statement. **A *whole* book.**

ERISA regulations do not cover State, Local, Federal and Church Pensions.

As an employer you can set up a 401k plan for your employees.

You will match what the employee puts into the fund. A usual employer match might be between 3% and 6% of an employee's salary.

THERE IS a limit to how much can be put in. The max. you are allowed to put in **2020** to a 401k (as an employee) is

$19,500. That is $500.00 more than 401k limit for 2019. See your tax accountant/fund manager on this.

401k are a good idea for employees especially when they can be self directed at times. 401k can be fully loaded into stocks, bonds or cash. See you tax professional on this self- directing.

Some people have regretted having their 401k loaded with stocks though, especially here in April/May 2020. Diversification may be needed.

In some situations Self-directing can be done into some real estate funds.

BONDS

Bonds are more conservative and safer for the investor. Stocks in general are riskier for the investor.

And Vice Versa, the bond is more risk for the company issuing them, and stock is less risky for the company.

The bond issuing company/city guarantees your initial investment back with additional varying interest rates.

On US TREASURY Bonds, which I do have a few, they are a guaranteed return by the US Government.

I bought them for half of Face Value, 1k FV and they have a maturity date of 20 years.

There is a max amount you can buy per year of these type of bonds, its 20k Face Value.

Governments, Cities, states or credit unions or large companies issue bonds. Bonds usually have a maturity date at which the full value of it has been achieved. 10 to 20-30 years max. Normally when a bond matures its full face value can be exchanged at a bank.

Normally Bonds pay interest once or twice a year at varying rates, in years past average dividend has been about 4-6%.

But In the past year 2019, the 10 year US Treasury bonds have not cracked 2% return. As of May 3 2020 a 10 year Treasury yield rate is 0.7 percent, not even one percent. Not good and not the type of bond I currently recommend.

T-bills and T-notes are different securities with typically shorter maturity times, like 52 weeks or less.

In a recent article by **Aaron Gregg** and **Christian Davenport**, The Washington Post

May 1, 2020 at 1:11 p.m. PDT

"Boeing has raised $25 billion in a massive debt sale, allowing it to avoid tapping a $17 billion Coronavirus bailout fund meant to shore up businesses critical to national security.

> *The bond sale significantly increases Boeing's chances of riding out the crisis without direct government support. Turning down the funds means the company will not have to give the government an ownership stake, a requirement that executives had said they wouldn't accept."*

This is **very** important. It shows you one Major US company who is disagreeing with the government owning part of it/ getting equity, in exchange for the 2020 bailout.

Which if you didn't know, is one of the main parts of socialism/communism, where the government owns business, no private owned trade/business.

This 25 Billion in Boeing bonds was at 5% dividend return. The bonds sold out in 72 hours. Five percent return on 25 billion is 1 Billion 250 million. Big money, moving fast.

ETFS.

ETF = 'Exchange-traded fund'

The **ETF** works like this: The fund provider designs the group of securities and offers it thru brokers. **ETFs are traded** daily on the exchange, like a stock.

Some ETFs have bonds or commodities or precious metals in them and some have Real Estate in REITs. Similar to mutual funds, but the generally lower fees and tax advantages are more attractive in ETFs.

Some ETFs have gold and silver in them but it is just a leased commodity and you never really see it.

Owning Gold and Having an ETF in gold, *is not the same thing.*

> "Keep in mind that you do not own any physical gold even if you invest in a physically-backed ETF: you cannot redeem or sell shares in exchange for gold."
>
> — FROM INVESTOPEDIA.COM/ARTICLES

Once again these are based on the stock market and go up and down just like other stocks. I do not do ETF investing.

REITS.

I'm going to move on here to the REITs, the Real Estate Investment Trust.

These are something I don't recommend either but I will explain to you how they're different than investing with a partner or buying properties on your own.

REITs are stock that you are purchasing and so you are not actually a partner in the deal, and you **do not** get to take the depreciation of the real estate with a Tax Schedule K1.

Tax form Schedule K1. It includes losses, gains, depreciation, that's the IRS form where that's filled out. If you have a home or investment property your taxman will/should do this for you.

A REITs value is based on the stock market so when the stock market goes down, it goes down.

Most of these REITS that I have seen you do get interest/residual payments but only every 3 months, not every month like an actual apartment building does.

Some of the REITS I have been offered have been based on commercial real estate like a shopping center or a Rite Aid tenant. Not what I'm looking for in commercial real estate.

When you own part (shares) of a REIT and the owners are refinancing the building(s) that the REIT is based on, you usually would get your dividend but not a piece of the equity (the real prize in multi- family investing and SFR). Dividends are NOT guaranteed also (see your prospectus).

REITS pay you Dividends on taxable income from the properties. Money gotten out OF THE PROPERTY on refinancing is NOT Taxable Income.

I do **not** recommend REITS, especially when they are commercial buildings, with one or a few tenants.

Recently with the Covid 19 Quarantine and in this day and age, work at home, even for a large corporation is happening more and more. Office space is needed less and less. Social distancing is "safer".

A "new normal" is being promoted and the office building/cubicle is less part of it.

SILVER AND GOLD

> "In 1971, president Nixon took the US dollar off the Gold Standard. In 1971, the US dollar became fiat money. "Fiat" money is government money. Rich dad called government money "fake money". Fake money makes the rich richer. The problem is that fake money makes the poor and middle class poorer"
>
> — ROBERT KYOSAKI, FAKE : MONEY, TEACHERS, ASSETS.

Since 1971 the US Govt. has created *Trillions* of dollars in Debt because it was free to do that, not being tied to the GOLD standard anymore.

In 1933 President Roosevelt made it illegal for any Americans to own Gold, In 1974 Pres. Ford repealed this and made it legal to own Gold.

For me, Gold and Silver are not really investments. I think of it as insurance in case of bank breakdown etc. But they do appreciate. I own Gold and Silver, I am not investing in it.

PROS

I like this Gold and Silver for a few reasons:

If the banking system breaks down, almost all people trust Gold and Silver. Even if it's a coin from South Africa, its still 1 ounce of pure Silver and it says so on the coin usually.

It was here when we started and It will be here when we leave.

It has staying value.

It will not get eaten by rats or cockroaches. Pablo Escobar, famous drug cartel, had so much cash, storage was a real problem and rats ate 1 Billion in cash EACH YEAR.

Very little risk. The real Gold, (not gold in ETFs) is holding and increasing in value, The US dollar is losing value constantly, going to down to zero eventually.

Gold and Silver in an ETF is leased, not owned by you.

Gold and Silver cannot be manipulated as easily by Wall Street people or The Elites who rule the country.

> "Paper money has had the effect in your State that it ever will have, to ruin commerce, oppress the honest, and open a door to every species of fraud and injustice."
>
> — GEORGE WASHINGTON

CONS

Gold and Silver, are not liquid like digits are, or dollars/crypto etc. You can't carry it around very easily, especially Silver, its value is much much less than Gold. May 8 2020 Silver is at $15 dollars an ounce. Gold is at $1717 an ounce.

Safely storing the Gold/Silver can be a problem, I definitely don't recommend a bank.

The Gold/Silver you buy can be tainted/impure, it is generally safe but you need to know who you are buying from.

I do recommend investing in this, but not high on my scale of senior investments at the end of this chapter. Silver can be much easier to start with, as its much more affordable. Gold is available in 1/10th of an ounce coins currently at about $220 each.

"Specie [gold and silver coin] is the most perfect medium because it will preserve its own level; because, having intrinsic and universal value, it can never die in our hands, and it is the surest resource of reliance in time of war."

— THOMAS JEFFERSON APRIL 13, 1743 – JULY 4, 1826. 3RD PRESIDENT OF THE USA.

WARNING, I do not recommend numismatic "rare" coin purchases, unless you are an expert in this. You can easily pay too much for a 1922 US Silver dollar and get taken advantage of, when you just want the .999 fine Silver coin. Recent dates with 1 ounce Silver coins is fine. South African Krugerrands are good, Us Silver Eagles are good. Canadian dollars before 1966 are good, only .80% silver though. Chinese Pandas (30 grams) are ok too. 28.4 grams in an ounce.

I will probably write another book just on this topic, Silver and Gold, its importance is growing as the classes get further apart.

THE IRA AND SEP

The SEP stands for Simplified Employee Pension. This is the common IRA(Individual Retirement Account) used by self-employed and small business owners.

If you have The SEP it allows you to contribute much more than a standard IRA, which is $6000 annually 7k if you're over 50y/o.

The SEP IRA allows you to contribute more, up to 25% of your annual wages up to $57000 total per year. There are other IRS guidelines for you to consider regarding SEP IRA. https://www.irs.gov/retirement-plans/retirement-plans-faqs-regarding-seps.

The SEP IRA can be converted to a self directed IRA, and invested in other things besides, the usual stock, bonds mutual funds and ETFs. The whole thing can be converted or just a portion of it. This self-directing is one way to get into other types of investing products such as

1. Commercial Real Estate
2. Precious metals
3. Private lending
4. Tax liens, notes
5. Buying your own business
6. Crypto, and Forex

and more are allowed.

There are a few things not allowed, Such as:

1. Real estate for non commercial/living use
2. Gems, Art, metal
3. Alcohol

And others.

BOTTOM LINE, WHAT DOES BRETT RECOMMEND ?

If you asked me a scale of what to invest in from best to worst, I would list it as:

1. *Multi family apartment housing above 15 units.*
2. *Real estate such as housing that is distressed where you make make money on the purchase (automatic equity).*
3. *Gold/Silver 3A.Crypto Currency*
4. *Bonds.*
5. *ETFs.*
6. *Stocks. Mutual Funds.*

When I look at this list, it really is easiest/most affordable to start at #6 and seemingly the toughest to get into number #1, especially for the little guy/beginner.

But Crypto, Silver and Gold actually are very easy to get into too, EBAY has reputable Bullion sellers. And Real estate in the USA is opening up for the investor.

And if I can do it, so can you.

BCL

COLLEGE, COURSES AND ONLINE BUSINESSES

Okay now I'm going to go into talking about college, taking courses and online businesses to make money with.

Now I personally did not finish college (attended Virginia, NOVA community college, one year). I did start and studied Music and Psychology. I wanted to write music and be in a band which I did from 1990 to near present day.

I am not a person that recommends going to college unless you're going to become a doctor or a lawyer or an engineer with serious technical data and knowledge where peoples lives are bet/risked on your knowledge/ability.

College produces average people geared towards only being employees and possibly self employed. It is *Not* really creating Big business or Investors.

Don't get me wrong, I'm still an employee at a non-profit part-time and some employees do make a very good living. That's just not my end goal though, to be an employee.

If you're going to go to college, go to the Ivy league, Yale, Princeton etc., go to meet the next President or the next Senator of your state and make the contacts of a lifetime. Networking. Contacts. Very Important.

The other thing I don't like about college is that usually you end up owing a bunch of money to the government.

It easily can be 100s of thousands of dollars and I even have heard of an orthodontist who owed over a million dollars!

The Schools Product, (you), and what you come away with is not the important essential things regarding money, investments, sales, and practical experience teaching, like this book and real world experience.

"My accounting teacher was not a real accountant. He had no real life experience. He required us to listen to him talk, memorize his answers, take his tests, and not make mistakes. He was a Fake teacher."

— FROM ROBERT KYOSAKI'S, FAKE MONEY, FAKE TEACHERS, FAKE ASSETS.

EMPLOYEE

If you wanted to become a nurse you don't have to go to college.

You could go to one of these one or two year "career colleges" there's many of them around, especially here in Los Angeles.

Its half the time and then you're out there in the workforce making money, helping the community and pushing the grind wheel of EXPERIENCE.

I know what my four kids went thru in school, my youngest is in college now at 20y/o. She will be a nurse or doctor possibly.

I know what I know from school and then my 32 years Experience in the Real world practice. I value the Real world practice and Success more.

Example:

I went to a 13 month long computer school "Computer Learning Center" in Los Angeles, 1999. I used a Federal student loan, and borrowed close to 20k. The CLC company went bankrupt 5 days after the last class. ALL 5 or 6 plus campuses it had, closed down.

Separate from the schooling (on my own), I did The "MCSE" certification. "Microsoft Certified System Engineer".

This MCSE was not easy and cost me about $600 cash extra and was 6 different tests. I thought it would set me apart from the average worker or applicant when it came time to be employed in computers. I was also working part time with a programmer helping different companies run their computer network, good experience; but not enough.

With less than a years experience in the computer field, 13 months CLC and this MCSE certificate, I was not employable. I went to a few unsuccessful interviews after graduation. The school promised employment, one of the main reasons I signed up. No dice. Promise broken.

I did not get a job or make it in that field and instead continued to build my Airfresh company which I was involved with also at that time.

One big thing I learned about this computer school/college experience was that experience in the field is a *HUGE* factor and your diploma or certification was not that important really. That's what the employers told me basically. 2 years real world/job experience they wanted to see.

College does not give you a financial education, or show you how to sell, or how to invest and how to pay the least taxes. They mostly really teach you how to be an employee, which pay a lot of taxes. The little college practical application you get, cannot be counted as real-world experience and it is not, mostly.

Apprenticeships are lacking or missing entirely.

The above points may not be the case with all, **but most** schooling.

Unfortunately Teaching is one of the worst paid professions. And paying even more money to the teacher is not going to solve the situation.

The right study technology (how to study), gradient, curricula and practical applications, *is*.

"Companies are all math. They are legal entities. They don't care or have feelings. A company can never love you.

So if you don't have the ability to provide for yourself, or depend on only yourself for your income, what do you have?"

— THE MIKKELSEN TWINS, ONLINE BOOK PUBLISHERS

You should know how to provide for yourself, you are a business. Your name and your reputation is a brand. They can take your money away but not your brand. Protect it.

This book shows you some key parts of that.

> *"If money is your hope for independence you will never have it. The only real security that a man will have in this world is a reserve of knowledge, experience, and ability."*
>
> — HENRY FORD - BUSINESSMAN (1863 - 1947)

There is one more viewpoint on employee that I would put out, that is that you are making someone else's dream come true and forwarding their goals to their expansion.

Nothing wrong with that on the way to acquiring your own assets, this steady income is going to be needed to some large or smaller degree.

Employee can be fruitful *but,* big passive income and the big tax advantages lie in having corporations and other business entities that protect assets such as real estate.

Having your own corporation/LLC etc. is not going to involve being an employee usually, however with your own business or properties, it can.

YOUTUBE. ONLINE TEACHERS

Also from the book FAKE, from Robert Kyosaki

"the best teachers are on Youtube, not in schools"

I completely agree with RK on this. The videos can show you anything from how to build a house, to change your car headlight, to invest money properly (where you don't lose it).

There is an abundance of technology on Youtube, current, money making technology and businesses and a lot of them show you the check$ for proof. A small amount of these are legit.

Sorting the true from false and whats right for you and your skillset, is the hard part of Youtube. Some are fly by night "opportunities".

Example: "Amazon Automation businesses"I've seen one Personality promoting this on youtube, they ask for 30 k+ per year FEE and 50% of your profit. They use "VAs" (virtual assistants) in Bangladesh or the Phillipines who handle the whole business for you essentially, running your Amazon store.

A lot of this is drop shipping from Wal-mart. More than likely the pitch is scamming/deceiving the customer w/the 30k. In this game you need abundance because without it, the profit won't be enough to justify the investment.

Regarding the above example for buying products you also (in addition to the 30k fee) need a credit card with 20-50 k available on it to reach a profit of near ten percent (5k), but then you will split that with your partner?,not good.

Some of these are legit, some are not and none will be something that's been in business for a long time.

(Drop-shipping is where you are the retailer, getting the sale thru your store on Amazon, Shopify or other online connection and the supplier (Wal mart etc.) supplys and ships it for you to the customer).

There is a bit more to it that I didn't mention, some is the large WORK that the VA's do for you.

And then you have books like this which are among the cheapest and quickest ways to find out how to make some money or how to **not** make the mistakes that successful people have made. This book is a collection of professional details that set you apart from the rest.

Some people value mistakes highly and encourage them, saying

"you can learn from them".

I do not want you to learn about real estate and investing by losing your money, any of it.

I particularly in our company investigate mistakes and look for what should **NOT** be there. Mistakes can be used as a bad indicator.

The number one thing is do. The sale you never try, never gets sold, for sure.

If it it's not quite right, ok, you are not a pro yet. *But you are doing.*

ONLINE BUSINESSES, THE SIDE HUSTLE.

Everyone has a friend that has "the plan" and gets involved with one or more of these below :

- Growing an Instagram page
- Buying and selling domain names
- Network marketing
- Blogging
- Flipping houses
- Starting a podcast
- Buying and selling on eBay
- Starting a YouTube channel

And sometimes it works out, but most of the time not, due to a few factors.

Some are:

- Improper estimation of effort needed
- Not enough promotion of it
- They are trying to "game the system" and get shut down
- Not thinking big enough
- Selling/promoting a product that is not wanted/needed
- And not knowing how to sell.

And other factors that could have some reality such as if "I could just get enough capital" which is true of any business for easier, rapid expansion.

AMAZON SALES

Online businesses is a whole book in itself.

Now some of my personal experience with this is as follows.

Circa 2018, so me and my wife talk about going into sales on Amazon, of course I start looking at Youtube and found Amazon Pro, Seth Kniep.

I liked his focus, drive and the course price compared to other courses was a bit lower.

So, me and my wife in 2018 purchased a course that cost about $1,200 from a company called Just One Dime (JOD) with Seth Kniep, mister " Kniepn it real."

Now I can't really recommend the course because I never actually went and bought a product and sold it on Amazon and did not really finish the course fully but I will tell you my experience with it because I did quite *a lot* of work on it.

I did about 150 hours of study, emails, calls and research.

(The course turned out to be only a membership which expired in 2019) :(

On the "course", most of the research I did to find a good product to sell was on a program called "AmazeOwl" and on then supplying the actual product was through alibaba.com and aliexpress.com. As recommended by the course.

A feature I did like about the course was the private facebook group(s) created just for members of JOD. These groups had a lot of activity, encouraging helpful advice, review swap and could help launch your New product!

These Ali websites above are going to connect you with suppliers that produce products in China, India, Malaysia and other Far East places like that where you are going to want to order them. You then get your product custom designed to whatever specifications or brand name you create then get them produced. Of course you want to buy them in bulk for the best pricing and then you're going to be selling them on FBA (fulfilled by Amazon) and have your own Amazon store.!

Sounds simple enough.

You would have the product then shipped from Asia to the FBA distribution centers (which there is many in the USA now, 5 in California alone) where you store the product until sold. You do pay for the storage of your product also by the way.

The shipping procedures can be a whole book or definitely a chapter. Boats, Air, Trains, Customs Fees etc. There's a bit to know about shipping your product.

Now I never made it to that point of selling an actual product,

I almost did, doing some test runs to see the quality of some of the Chinese products but I decided against selling on Amazon and partly the reason I did was because I already had a business that I was doing and it was pretty successful.

This FBA research/calls were taking a lot of my time and was going to take a good amount of money to invest in (about 3k to start) and FBA was not a successful action from my past.

Also for me, the "straw that broke the FBA camel's back" and made me say

"no, I'm not going to do this right now" (which I still haven't completely decided I will never do it again),

Was that the rules that Amazon FBA runs by are changed whenever they want or see fit : the JOD course and its launch program became unusable, for whatever reasons.

The launch of an Amazon product is very important, the whole launch guidelines through the JOD course changed while I was studying it, though this course was pretty informative and in it they had a" Facebook Launch group" just created to help you launch the products. (I believe that group was disbanded due to infringement of Amazon terms)

In the group, you would purchase other people's products and help them by leaving a positive review and it was laid out in a way to help you as well on your launch, but unfortunately a lot of that stuff is not available or allowed to be done anymore on FBA, as far as I've seen.

July 2020, I am not up-to-date as to what they're current TOS (term of service Agreements) are for fulfilled by Amazon, FBA.

This JOD "course" mainly covered private label where you buy some products from Alibaba.com and slap your label on "your brand", and then sell it on Amazon, Shopify etc.

A lot of people have done FBA successfully in this model and I know one personally, he did the "Amazing Sales Machine" course about 5 years ago.

The Course cost was near 5k then and it has worked out for him selling pet products.

He does it as a "side hustle" and has a full time job. Last stat I heard from him was like 15k in sales in April 2020. That's pretty good stats, especially for Covid 19 quarantine time production.

RA

Then there is RA (Retail Arbitrage). Yes that's where you're buying Amazon approved products (which change frequently like certain products are not allowed to be resold) you buy a bunch of them cheaply at Kmart or Walmart etc, and then you resell them on Amazon at a profit.

With RA, there's many products they do not allow you to do that with like Disney products, Nike Etc. You must be an authorized dealer for some products.

> "Amazon requires items sold as new to carry the original manufacturer's warranty. This is where RA becomes an issue because most manufacturer's do not provide a warranty for items sold by a third party. To be on the safe side of things for RA new items should be listed as used like new to be in compliance with Amazon policies."
>
> — FEB 2019 - FROM GIZMO 192 ON SELLERCENTRAL AMAZON.COM

This above quote is not entirely true, most manufacturers do provide warranty to 3rd parties on new items sold.

Takeaway from this chapter, a course, college or Amazon, you are still trying to build a business. Even if it's just you. Build yourself first and go out from there.

BCL

RECESSIONS, DEPRESSIONS, PANDEMICS

Recessions, Pandemics, Depressions, and making it THRU.

Ok.

The American Heritage dictionary second edition defines recession as "*a moderate and temporary decline in economic activity*".

This is derived from Latin recesivo which comes from the word recess "*a temporary cessation of customer activities*, occupation or pursuit "

From same America Heritage dictionary Depression "*a period of drastic decline in the national economy, characterized by decreasing business activity falling prices and unemployment.*"

Right here April 2020, I would call this a Depression.

Gas prices in the south near .80 cents a gallon.

Unemployment is at 35 million (there is 328 million total people in USA).

All sports, movie theaters, malls, most "unessential business" closed down.

Restaurants are allowed to only have drive thru and take out. (August 2020, this is still continuing in California).

So whatever the normal customer things are going on they have stopped economically that would be a recession. But currently THIS APRIL 2020 is beyond that.

What's the Handling for this?

ACCEPTANCE

> *"Five stages: denial, anger, bargaining, depression and **acceptance** are a part of the framework that makes up our learning to live with the one we lost. They are tools to help us frame and identify what we may be feeling. But they are not stops on some linear timeline in grief."*
>
> — QUOTE FROM WWW.GRIEF.COM

April 2020, There is an Economic Depression/disaster.

And you will some way, somehow have to make it up to ACCEPTANCE on this list.

This Covid 19 was not immediately accepted by everyone, as a health concern or especially as an **ECONOMIC DISASTER**.

Some said "Its nothing" just the flu.

Some said "they are infringing on my 1st Amend. rights" angrily.

Some said "Help me out of this God, and I will be a good boy and go to church every Sunday"

Some Said "F' it were done, I give up" and promptly started drinking heavily.

But Some said, "okay its here, what can we do today about it "and did it. For weeks and months. I'm still pushing out our products here in June 2020.

That last statement, I said that and *Believe* me this 2020 March, April, May, was tough even for me.

I will cover that more, but right now I just want to go over what are the immediate actions you would want to take in a Recession/Depression /crisis.

Well first you would need to come to acceptance with it and you would have to accept the fact that things are not the same and if you continue to do the same things, it is not going to be pretty.

What I have found in 20 years of Contracting here going through 2008, 2020 here at least two different recessions for sure is that whatever amount your business is doing of promotion or Facebook ads, letters or emails, etc. you're going to *need triple* that amount to do that same amount of business that you were doing before that bad area, crisis, recession started.

3x your promotion.

The next comment I will make is, let's say you start that 3x in your promotion and you do a week of it and you do another week and another week.

Good, don't expect to see any results until about 4 to 6 weeks later, to see a rise in the graphs of income, jobs being done, products being sold etc.

Whatever it is, there is going to be a bit of a lag. It's not always going to be an immediate response when you start Pushing the 3x.

Pretend you got nothing.

The next step in the recession/Depression handling is going broke and what I mean by that is I don't care if you got 100 grand in the bank or your 401k.

You gotta pretend you got nothing, or else you'll get lazy and spend too much and that's not going to get your business UP to the top. 100 grand comparatively is nothing and your 401k, that needs to be put/kept to use in assets, long term.

To Quote Nerdwallet.com

"Typically, the penalty for withdrawing from a 401(k) before the age of 59½ is 10% of the distribution, plus an automatic withholding of at least 20% for taxes. But with the passage of the CARES Act, that all changes in 2020.

...the CARES Act's language on early withdrawals from retirement accounts is remarkable in itself.

Here's a broad overview: Individuals affected by COVID-19 can withdraw up to $100,000 from employee-sponsored retirement accounts like 401(k)s and 403(b)s, as well as personal retirement accounts, such as traditional individual retirement accounts, or a combination of these.

- *The 10% penalty will be waived for distributions made in 2020.*

- *There are no mandatory withholding requirements."*

Resource: https://www.nerdwallet.com/blog/investing/cashing-out-401k-covid-19/

See your Tax professional on this. I am not a CPA and this is very fluid, changing weekly/monthly in California/USA.

In the middle of a depression, if you had one of these 401ks stuffed with funds great, but most of us reading this probably do not and **should be out there producing, regardless.**

LIABILITIES, THAT WERE ASSETS. VICE VERSA.

The next move in the company or in your life is deciding what is an asset and what's a liability. Crisis brings change.

To give an example like let's say you own a cleaning company like me and your company contracts out cleaning services for a client and you get a call from the client saying "hey look we have to cancel our contract for right now cause of Covid 19 ".

Well you've got to preemptively strike and renegotiate that deal and say "look you know we understand the situation with (covid 19, recession) we're going to lower the contract to one year instead of two that was left on it and give you a couple of free months and the next couple of months you can not pay the full payment "This will keep some damage from occurring to your business.

That contract was an asset but then the recession or the pandemic hits now it's become a bit of a liability and it's got to be restructured.

I just want to reiterate the word "liability', specifically its meaning :

"something that causes more harm than good"

So that could be financially, that could be socially, that could be in your business in the smoothness of its running, these kind of things come up every day and especially in crisis situations.

One BIG liability here in 2020, is the News and "fake media" and the focusing/listening on it too much. Especially something long lasting like this Pandemic, an inundation of Bad News.

Social media, Facebook, Instagram, limit your intake of it, or eliminate if you can, especially in times of trouble. Limiting your total TV intake to only weekends is going to give your more time to produce/work. I watch very little Netflix etc.

I recommend in any crisis situation, limit your intake of this media. It can be too much for some people, News influencing them VERY negatively. "The sky is falling!" "you will get sick "etc.

I never met or heard of anyone that said "the media saved my life".

This can be HUGE and should NOT be underestimated at all.

What you focus on/ put your attention on gets power.

PERFECTIONISM

The next Viewpoint you would want to look at here is perfectionism.

Being in a recession, pandemic etc. is not the time to be pushing perfectionism.

You need to change and to be the change.

> *"to change you must give something up.* Getting rid of something old or questionable makes room for something new.
>
> There is no change by simply adding new behaviors or information.
>
> Change requires you surrender something first."
>
> — GRANT CARDONE ON THE PANDEMIC
> APR 2020

That can mean **a lot** here. You need to give something up.

In life, Could be your drinking on the weekend, partying, could be the crowd you've been hanging with. Taking drugs. (I was a teen druggie, I know all about that junk). Could be watching TV too much.

Examples: In Business possibly that means

- Working an area that's not your expertise, working for a lower price,
- Change in the product price,
- Change in the contract,
- Leave the current strategy and adopting a new radical one.

- Furlough or Dropping employees or equipment.
- All spending gets approved by the top first. All.
- TRIPLING or Quadrupling your promotional Budget.
- Temporarily Cutting ALL employees pay structure.

The perfectionism is not something you want to stick with at that crisis point.

You could lose some valuable contacts, contracts, sales or workers in your organization, if you are trying to be perfect at a crucial make/break point some crisis can create.

Example, the client normally has you do so much work on this routine maintenance,but now they cannot afford it, so you alter the service and price.

Example, collections are very slow from one client who normally pays 30 days; you would let them be late, very late if needed, not even think about legal collections. You would keep in communication with them and work it out, maybe even offer a settlement price as last resort, or a "buy now" deal to get a flow going. Possibly give them 12 months service for ten months price.

Example, you get a call from a customer and they tell you a complaint from a job done three months ago. You could brush it off, because they were one of the worst customers ever and you feel you've done all that can be done on the job.

But right now you handle that origination somehow, even if you have to go out there again to do it. Sometimes just showing up and looking is enough to handle the complaint.

SPENDING, YOUR LIFE AND BUSINESS. DISCIPLINE.

March 2020, Right away I was stopping spending in the company as soon as these stay at home orders were issued here in California. I furloughed some employees and staved off a few creditors.

In the household I told my wife also, no spending extra on the credit cards and on mortgage payments which she usually does. No shoes, no large payments without ok.

The discipline fully applies to your day and your time also. I personally was going to bed earlier, 9pm, getting up 8am, eat, workout, study till noon, eat then work til 5-6 pm at the job site or in the office, then after 6pm eat and work on this book.

That is my schedule during this quarantine. Every day.

This schedule may seem a bit lax, but it worked, and I forgot to add a few things in there, such as honey time and family time, as we have lots of brothers and sisters here and one kid still living at home.

Keeping the schedule in 15 min or 30 min slots is smart. It exerts control over time also, *which might be your most valuable possession or thing you create.*

Also Intake of tv, Facebook and news radio down to a minimum. Especially the news/radio,all of it is/was negative. Some people get very lit up by it.

The discipline can definitely involve who you talk to or don't. If he can't make me any money, lets skip it for now.

Example: Your friends want to get together and drink, and you know you should be working. Discipline.
Example :You want to play drums in a band, its fun but there's no money in it and your Family and job start to suffer because of it. It can be tough, I've done it. (not playing drums though)

Discipline, focusing on money making activity and things that are more important.

SPENDING

In a Depression/recession there is usually going to be a Govt. bailout of some type, "Stimulus check", PPP etc. (see Ch 9.) But how should you spend that stimulus money or the money you have during the crisis?

My Spending Model

If its gonna make money soon for sure. Do it.

Example: PAST PROVEN Successful Promotion for your business, or buying equipment to get a job done, for a job **that is SOLD**. Do it.

If its likely to make money, possibly ok.

Example: affiliate marketing course, Amazon FBA crse, your book. Real estate course. These are all usually tax deductible.

If its not immediately going to make money and its risky, speculative (stocks, penny stock delusions of grandeur). Don't do it.

New Skiis/Snowboard, vintage wine, a new Gucci bag. Don't do it.

Example: You know you should save/invest the money but instead you buy some guitars. Cool, especially if they are going to be used for a paycheck soon.

You probably shouldn't be talking a deal with that Guitar Center guy unless there is a paying gig with that Guitar. Don't do it.

If its a tax deductible expenditure, that's a good sign such as a sales course or postage for promotional mail, or promotional swag for your trade show, customers etc.

Do it.

In crisis, at some point you might want to only spend on tax deductible items.

A word on promotion for our company during the Covid 19 QUARANTINE, I only slowed one area of promotion, some billboards we had out, we suspended till work resumed in the city June 2020. All other areas in promotion, we 3xd what we had been doing normally before Covid 19.

Takeaway from the chapter: This isn't the last emergency that will happen.

Depressions, Recessions etc. can be outcreated.

No virus can stop us.

BCL

7

SALES, IN BUSINESS AND LIFE.

Now this can be a whole book of itself but I'm just going to give one chapter of it here and refer to it a little bit here and there with my most successful actions from my company and life in Sales.

Number one would be what I would call referrals now this is one of the easiest sales because all you're doing is kind of just taking the Referral from another company or a customer and they are probably 99% sold when you pick up the phone with them and you're just sealing it with the right price and your good manners, yes! Easy sale, okay good.

Especially when you've already worked with the referring company an agreed on flow starts to happen.

Now I'm going to talk about this a little bit more though because this is very important now in any business area. What can be a Referral?

Well obviously another customer (Word of Mouth) but specifically other contractors. We work under other contractors all the time. Other AC contractors other General Contractors and other trades, and once you do one job for them you just keep in touch with them on a mailing list and phone calls every once in a while and you will get a job just like finding gold behind your house or something, there you go!

This is *really important*, it can actually make or break a business.

We used to pay a commission to these companies that referred us jobs but unfortunately the CA State Licensing Board sent us a warning about that many years ago, so we stopped doing that.

But in your non-construction business that is not governed by CSLB you probably could give a referral fee to them, 10% is a pretty standard amount.

I don't know about in your state but in this area you would be looking for trouble if you're giving them a construction referral fee in the state of California.

Ask you accountant for more legal specifics on this.

Word of Mouth referral is actually a jewel because the client is sold by the other customer for you!

CRM

The next definite most easiest sale for you to make, absolutely, positively as one of your general Business Basics have to have a list of all prior customers on computer, some type of mailing list/contact software CRM (Customer relationship management software).

Such as Service Titan, or Housecall Pro. It can help automate your business, by doing:

1. Texting the customer with the technicians picture and arrival time.
2. Help the technician close more jobs and make more money for him and you.
3. Keep track of your promotional ads and which ones with separate phone numbers are doing well or not.

There are many CRMs out there for you to try and some are more expensive than others. Some have monthly fees also. But a CRM can push your contracting/service business into overdrive!

There are CRMs such as Mycase.com for lawyers and Pipedrive.com for other fields too, not just for Contractors.

MAIL

In the CRM is the phone number, their USPS address, and email, fax etc.

You need to mail to it regularly 3x a year or more and you need to call them and service/maintain these addresses regularly. This is very important. It continues the connection. It keeps you in mind. "Out of sight out of mind". **Even the regular USPS mail, mail to it every 3-4 months. This is more important and more successful than email.**

A lot of jobs we do require maintenance in the cleaning field. If you're a lawyer they're going to have some need of a Living Trust and maybe need to do later another Power of Attorney or a Will or other legal cycle. If you're an artist you can send copies/samples of your newest work.

Selling to the customer that you've already done work for/sold is much easier than cold calls or people you've never done work for because you already have a rapport with them obviously, they might even remember you. There is already some agreement with your product, service or just you.

Selling the work again at a higher rate years later is easier to do because they know already it was $100 two years ago now it's $150, okay fine. Cost of living adjustment.

Your past customers are your **Contact Base** and it should be regularly maintained and updated with the addresses corrected and regular phone calls to it offering all your different products or same product/services again.

THE CONTACT BASE. IT IS GOLD.

Literally, I understood this one day when I was calling an invoice/customer from

13 years ago we did, and I resold him some work.

The 13 year old carbon/invoice is Goldenrod color!!

If you decide to come up with a different product or opportunity you have a ready-made list of people that you've already sold something to and trying to sell something similar or completely different even, will be easier.

This can include email addresses, phone numbers, fax numbers and addresses for USPS mail. Cell and text to cell, are very important especially in the service business.

THE SALE

I'm going to cover some of the parts of a sale.

THE GREETING

FIRST you have your contact, your first meeting with them. Always shake their hand if offered. Never refuse it. You want to create agreement.

Then you've got your manners. These are super important. It needs to be happy smiling and helpful. Dress code, it's got to look good, it's got to look appropriate to the environment you're in, if it's construction okay it can be casual jeans, but if it's an office, you know it needs to be clean, neat, no jeans and a suit possibly if its high end.

The attitude has to be friendly, helpful and welcoming. The chit-chat is ok but not necessary. **The shortest route to a sale is greet, offer a product and close, it can be as little as 10 seconds.**

Have you ever been to Home Depot in LA ? In their parking lot, in 10 seconds, a fruit salesman will offer you a free slice of orange.

You accept it and he pitches you the bag of oranges for 5$. That Fast.

SENIOR RULE OF SALES

"Agreeing with someone is senior to all other rules in selling "

Always, Always, Always, agree with the customer"

— GRANT CARDONE, SALES EXPERT

This is soo true it needs its own chapter. It's so powerful, it can diffuse almost any disagreement.

"Your price is too high", "I agree, just sign right there".

"You burned the dinner, its ruined" "I did. Lets go out to eat, my treat".

Even if what they say seems ridiculous, "I want no payments for 90 days and free insurance"

"We can do, I'm with you".

Diffuse anything with the agreement, it keeps the flow going, it keeps the yes going, it keeps the conversation going. Arguing, saying no, even correcting something he says in the conversation can be deadly and stop the flow.

This is something that should be drilled. Try it yourself, if you are not used to doing it like me, it can be diffucult. Try it for 24 hours, let me know how it goes.

Now in the conversation at some point you're going to have to present a product or service and ask them to buy it.

You have to ask for the sale, almost always you're not going to get any sale that you don't ask for.

In a non profit, which do I work for also in my off hours. In the asking for donations specifically, I like to not put out a number. I like to ask for donations and then see where they're at especially with people who are qualified to give thousands of dollars. Let them throw out a number. If after a bit, they don't, you can throw a suggestion their way.

You might have to ask them repeatedly in the same conversation. Ask as if you never asked before and you will be doing well.

This can take some drilling. Role playing sales is very helpful to learn the closes and the agreement.

It also puts you on the spot to do it smoothly, fast, without mistakes.

THE CLOSE.

> *"Of course, you could wait and not make a decision now, but I want to get it done so you can put your attention on things that are more important to you.*
>
> *Sign here and here please".*
>
> — GRANT CARDONE, THE CLOSER'S SURVIVAL GUIDE

Now when you are closing the deal there's many ways to do it, many ways, 100s, but the easiest is just to tell them "sign right here". (indicate with your hand) ------ Done. Good job.

Tell them what to do, and you both have it! Run the card and there you go or you deposit the check or contract with HQ.

On telling them what to do, some people react to this, emotionally.

Do not react yourself. Continue on the sale, agreeing all the way.

There are hundreds of different closes to use on people. You'll see them in action in car dealerships Nationwide, yes but the simpler you can keep it the better and the quicker ; people's attention spans these days get smaller and smaller.

The Close is *almost* the most important thing in Sales and deserves its own chapter and book.

Your job, the company, your pay and almost your life depend on it. The Close.

SALES IN LIFE, AND INVESTING

> "Do you want to end conflict? Then listen. Let them feel understood."
>
> — DEAN GRAZIOSI, AUTHOR, REAL ESTATE MILLIONAIRE

Now absolutely every single day you are selling yourself.

To your wife, to your kids, you want to get a date, to get her to go to the prom with you: you're going to have to sell.

You got to dress up, you got to be smooth and you got to ask for the close (marriage etc.)

You might be thinking "I'm already married to her, I closed the deal "yes, but you still have to keep creating the agreement in the group long after the "I do".

The agreement has to be continued and sold constantly, **to last**.

Successful people know how to sell and how to close.

Maybe they don't know it, but they're doing it and you're doing it to, I guarantee it.

It's just you haven't properly separated out into the specific parts, the sale, the close and been shown all the parts and then practiced it. You are creating agreement and yes, that is what marketing and sales is.

In life, give you an example here, let's say you go to a Medical Doctor and they say you (or your child) have some type of mental disorder like ADD or OCD or Bipolar, well they're going to say what they say: **but they're not going to show you any biological test that proves you have it.**

They are going to sell it though, in some way and you're either going to buy it or not. Its their *opinion*. Totally subjective.

This is a whole other book in itself, but unfortunately all those disorders in The DSM 5 (see glossary) ; No physiological test to prove anyone has any of the Disorders in DSM 5.

A Doctor MD, or Psychiatrist, Big Pharma, **selling /marketing** Disorders. Period.

See carefully how I did not say the word, *Disease*.

The point **is sales**. Are you buying? Are you selling ?

(If you would like more information on the facts of The DSM 5 and Disorders email me at the address at the end of this book.)

Absolutely, when you're a buyer, this applies also. When you go to buy a house or a multi-family building, you've got to create agreement that you are the one, you are qualified and you can manage the property. Its Sales, and in part Public Relations, which also needs its own chapter.

When you approach that owner with a proposal and your communications, it is all to sell you and your company/investors. The phone calls, the letters, proposals all form an opinion/agreement of who you are and what you want.

MEN AND WOMEN, SALES

Now with the wife, he brought her some flowers and some candy, yes HE'S trying to sell something there.

Maybe he's looking for a hot date, maybe they had a fight before I don't know but he's looking for some agreement and those presents and that niceness can sell him to her.

Yes, that flowers and candy are agreed to by a lot of women and mostly from men to women.

Yes, the men selling women seems to happen quite a lot more than the women selling the men, but it does happen that the women sell too.

Unfortunately, I don't know why men are selling more than women but that's a whole 'nother book also.

Now in my marriage I can sell my wife things, and I know I'm 100% sold on her. I am **Committed** to the relationship and the group and that builds a power base, which becomes stable.

You'll sell even more because of it, to her and others.

It creates harmony. It creates stability. It creates a firm executive structure for the family group. We are the leaders of the group.

Part of this is knowing what I'm responsible for and her knowing what she's responsible for. Part of it is completely trusting her and then being able to predict with her, our future.

Another Example:

I have three daughters and one is trying to find work currently (May 2020) at a local "juice" franchise. Now this is going to be competitive with millions unemployed currently, so I thought of something for her to say to guarantee they would hire her.

I said, *"you may not like this, but if you say it I guarantee they will hire you"*

So I continue, *"tell them, if you hire me I guarantee your sales stats will go up, I know how to sell, how to greet people, offer them a product/service, and how to close the deal, upsell and sell them an additional product on close. If you hire me and stats don't go up, you can fire me."*

Now that is selling yourself. SOLD, and now you'll have to deliver.

SENIOR DATA, ALL BUSINESS OWNERS WANT TO MAKE MORE MONEY.

You might think that is common knowledge, but from the employee viewpoint it is not common, but it will become important to you, if you want the business to do well and you to continue to have a job there.

This can apply to any job or department in the business:

HR (human resources): "I will hire the person who is well suited for the job and can make us more money."

Treasury: "I will collect more and keep our accounts in good credit standing so our credit is better."

Materiel/Equipment: "I will keep all the materiel in good order, maintained, therefore allowing us to use it longer and not need to spend money on newer equipment or repair etc."

SALES: FOLLOW UP

Now the follow-up in the sales department is super important. In my personal opinion it's not done enough from company to company I've seen.

I know I personally have sold jobs that have been on my books for years and years, even a decade and I still continue to follow up with them and chase down work or a specific job and then it finally turns into something.

The persistence is the key factor, if you want to make it in business you're going to have to learn how to persist, possibly to levels you are not accustomed to, such as I mentioned before, even a decade plus.

Not everything is going to happen overnight or right away with sales.

The follow-up can be for a job that you haven't sold and are still trying to sell or it also is used absolutely after a job/product is done to make sure everything's okay with the work and to prospect for other customers, or other work from the happy customer.

Selling that person more work now is even easier and they might refer a friend. Which happens all the time.

Doing the follow up for a first time sale is a good time to tag with another sales person, possibly since you so far have been unsuccessful with the sale. I have used my wife on some of these "tags" very successfully and with our technicians who are doing the job with upselling more work also.

Teaching your technicians the technology of sales is probably not being done in most companies and is VERY important. It can make you a lot more sales/money.

Bringing a tag in on a sale that is taking too long can help also, to close the deal by using a fresh face or reaffirming handling to the origination from the customer.

SALES AND BELIEVING IN YOUR PRODUCT/SERVICE.

Before you start a business and try to sell the product or the service I recommend picking something you are 100% sold on yourself, committed, and guaranteed to not waver on.

This would be like if you love music, well you're trying to sell music recording equipment or musical instruments or if you're a super car enthusiast and you want to be a car salesman for your favorite car maker.

You will run into trouble if you're not 100% sold yourself on the product or service. You are not committed fully. I have personal experience with this when I was selling chimney cleaning and chimney products for a company here in Los Angeles.

On that job, if you didn't sell when you were doing these chimney cleaning "sales calls "then you were making minimum wage and we all know that's not going to cut it. So you had to upsell, and find problems to handle with their chimney.

So, I wasn't myself 100% sold on setting someone up with a Chimney Cap. There was a sales pitch that you had to give to sell the cap. My uncertainty showed in my communication and my sales stats.

Also the chimney repairs we were trying to sell, some I felt were questionable, so I tended to try to sell something else or not focus on the repair enough, but the repairs were the big ticket item.

I ran into trouble, I had up and down days and unfortunately I didn't last more than about two years in the chimney business. I was a young man luckily but I did a lot of **Hard** work for a very little amount of money.

Tough lesson to learn, I ate a lot of chimney soot, because I couldn't figure out why I had trouble selling.

I didn't have any training on selling, that compounded the issue.

Sell yourself first, on whatever it is.

SALES RULES

Now in sales here are just a few practical tips and rules:

1. If you want to sell them something,

Do not get antagonistic, hostile, resentful, any of these type of attitudes. You will not sell anything to them. Even if what they are saying is incorrect/false.

2. Never say to the customer when you're trying to sell them "if you don't buy now you never will "or they say "we'll be back "and you say "sure" (sarcasm). You don't know that they won't and that's also negative and could create antagonism.

3. During your pitch and your close always keep your cool, never appear flustered or lose your poise, no matter what is said to you.

4. Tag. Handing the customer off to another sales associate or a manager can be a good idea. Called "the tag", it can save something that is going south with a fresh face or a different approach rather than just the same person grinding and grinding.

5. A lot of times "The price" that is set for your product or service very easily could be $1,000 higher or $500 lower especially for larger service-oriented contracts or items. Know your flexibility in price for that job/product well.

The number that is set on that service contract/item is very arbitrary

sometimes, so trying to be concrete about holding to it at all times is not necessarily the right thing always.

6. Keep your pipeline full,if you have more people to call and sell and

appointments setup, you won't start to feel like you must sell the one in front of you because you have no others to sell to or work with. Keep your calendar FULL.

7. Don't be afraid to raise your prices either,when things are going well or not so well.

8. You Must Must MUST regularly keep in contact with your past sold customers thru mailings and phone calls. Mailing to them 3 x year or more. (We do about 4). This keeps your addresses up to date for them also.

9. Always have an elevator pitch ready for impromptu meetings with the right people. (a quick smooth 20 second pitch).

Takeaway from the chapter;

Sell, and have the life you need and want.

BCL

8

GOVT. BAILOUTS, SBA LOANS, PPP, AND EIDL

Okay this chapter is going to cover the MARCH 2020 US government bailouts for Covid-19 crisis Etc this will include the PPP (paycheck Protection Program), EIDL, the SBA Loans/grants and the EDD.

These programs were created here in March 2020 as help for the small businessman like me and all the other people that have a business under 500 employees, which is a lot of businesses.

These type of programs have been available in the past like when the Northridge Earthquake came through here and my business was just up and running in the early 1990s.

I did not take advantage of any of those programs. Now, I definitely am taking advantage of it and I would highly recommend if you're reading this and anything like this happens again or in the later part of this year even. Some of these programs are available till the end of 2020. SBA.gov is where you start to look.

EIDL

The EIDL Economic Injury Disaster Loan (EIDL)-COVID-19 related assistance program (including EIDL Advances) is based on available appropriations funding.

This 10k loan was a grant, actually the first $10,000 forgivable as a grant as long as you're using it on rent, mortgage payments, Insurance, payroll. Initial Appropriations for it were gone approx 15 days after it was released. We received a one time grant of 1k thru this program in May 2020.

In the forgiveness, possibly I imagine you could show any receipt for anything to keep your business running and they would probably accept it.

After 10 grand, the loaned money is at 3.75% interest (a pretty haveable rate). Our company did get an SBA loan of 10k at 3.75 interest, payments starting 12 months after the loan began. They offered 30k to us.

PPP

Specifically the SBA.gov PPP loan paycheck Protection Program is being run through most websites for the banks/credit unions and they're taking a little while to get back to people. Weeks and even Months.

At this writing April 19th 2020 the Federal money for this program supposedly was all used up (350 Billion), to be replenished hopefully. As of April 29 It was replenished with another 310 billion in funding.

Regarding our companies PPP loan, we personally applied through five Banks, Chase, Wells Fargo, Skybridge/Circadian, Kabbage and Lendio but you're only allowed to accept one Paycheck Protection Program loan, so apply to as many banks as you want but you could only accept one PPP loan.

WE at the 11th hour of june 30th got funded for a measely $11k of the 80k we qualified for PPP money. The program ended officially on June 30th 2020.

I don't know which of the five banks we applied to went thru, but it got done.

It went thru *on intention*. I intended us to get it and never gave it up.

REGARDING CHASE BANK:

JP Morgan Chase Turns Its Back on Small Business Clients

May 1st, 2020 BY ERIC GROVES from ALIGNABLE

"Unfortunately, greed and self interest once again got the better of Chase when they decided, with all the confusion and distraction of a crashing economy, they'd rather sacrifice you, their small business clients, to take care of themselves and their biggest customers. **So I think that small businesses should bank elsewhere.** *I spoke with a number of Chase small business clients from across the country with long-term banking relationships with Chase (some dating back to the 1970s) to find out what really happened. And it's worse than you think—not only were their loans not processed, the branch offices they worked with were kept in the dark about what was happening. Many still not knowing, three weeks after submitting their applications, where they stand in line."*

As of May 3rd 2020 Chase, has not responded to Airfresh Duct Cleaning Companies PPP loan application. Update May 8th 2020, Chase responded declined "due to unable to verify employees" which is not what use the PPP is only for, it's for Independent contractors (1099s) also, which we sent verification also for, but they didn't see it or possibly care as above.

EDD

The Employment Development Department.

If you didn't know it, (our company pays into it but never had a UI claim till now) in USA California this is the organization that handles unemployment insurance claims, or UI.

With 36 million plus currently unemployed, lately here there's a lot of that UI going around and in April 2020, in an unprecedented move the EDD came up with PUA (Pandemic Unemployment Assistance).

This is a new govt. "free money" program for even Self-employed, Independent Contractors and Business Owners to apply for. This has never been available before.

Its not a lot of money, usually $600 to $900 a month, and its not going to last forever. But, It's better than starving, and currently many businesses are still not open here on AUG 15th 2020 in Los Angeles.

30 million others have applied for this UI here in the USA. Payments can last up to 26 weeks (6 months).It's a weekly report system and normally if you work for even $100 in the reported week you do not qualify for the UI payment. The rates vary with each person. You do have to be actively looking for work.

BAILOUTS. 2008 COLLAPSE

These 2020 US Government bailouts are not new and they have good precedent with the below TARP program of OCTOBER 2008.

"The Troubled Asset Relief Program (TARP) is a program of the US GOVT. to purchase toxic assets and equity from financial institutions to strengthen its financial sector that was passed by Congress and signed into law by Pres. George W Bush on October 3, 2008. It was a component of the government's measures in 2008 to address the subprime mortgage crisis."

— WIKIPEDIA MAY 4 2020

The keyword here in this above quote would be "equity". Well here that is meaning a form of stock, that secures the Treasuries financial investment. (See below quote from TARP ACT). Now it looks like this was a mostly successful "bailout" but it did sell part of the company to the US treasury, which if you remember from Chapter 5 in the Bonds section, a main part of socialism communism is the government owning all business, no free trade. Its a slippery slope.

The TARP program was instituted after the fall of Lehman Bros in Sept 2008.

Also from Wikipedia 4 May 2020 TARP, Protection of Government

1. Equity stakes

"The Act requires financial institutions selling assets to TARP to issue equity TARP warrants (a type of security that entitles its holder to purchase shares in the company issuing the security for a specific price), or equity or senior debt securities (for non-publicly listed companies) to the Treasury".

The above quote makes it clearly stated "Equity" in every business that received TARP 2008 bailout money. Receiving the Lions Share of the Bailout at the top of list was Fannie Mae and Freddie Mac and Wells Fargo, B of A, Chase Etc. About 95% of these receivers of the 2008 Bailout were financial institutions.

SEPTEMBER 2008 LEHMAN BROS COLLAPSED, WHAT HAPPENED?

First to understand what happened to Lehman Bros, you need to clear a few shadow banking terms. MBS (mortgage backed securities) and CDS (credit default swaps).

Mortgage Backed Securities are financial derivatives made of packaged mortgages sold together as a whole as an investment (security). They have different ratings, such as AAA, AA, A, BB,

B, C, Prime would be AAA, AA and A, subprime would be the lower letters.

CDS, credit default swap, a form of credit default insurance sold to insure the derivative holder ; someone like Lehman Bros. In that case Sept 2008, Lehman holding too much MBS insured with CDS. The MBS were full of subprime(but labeled prime falsely) loans. The MBS's were defaulting on Lehman and the payments were being called in by the CDS holders.

2008 Sept. Lehman was holding onto too much risky MBS and the SEC (Securities and Exchange Commission)and other regulating bodies knew they were. Knowing they were holding too much risky derivatives as early as 2007, the SEC looked the other way on it and did not require them to do anything effective about it.

Approximately 3 weeks later Oct 3 2008 GW BUSH POTUS bailed out all the other major financial institutions. Lehman Bros. was not saved. It was too late.

Takeaway from this chapter- In recessions, depressions, disaster etc. use these Govt. programs, apply for the money and follow the rules. I didn't in the past and I regretted it.

Also watch for the Bailout. It signals Billions-Trillions of dollars usually influxed into the economy, which has certain effects: Dollar going down, prices going up, moves towards socialism in Government owning businesses in part and more. - *BCL*

CRYPTO, BITCOIN: THE FUTURE OF A BUBBLE

What is Bitcoin? What it is based on? Why are we even talking about it?

On the aftermath of 2008 recession, somebody came up with an idea, a crazy idea...

Why don't we create a sort of mean to escape the traps of institutional banking?

A system that allows exchange of funds among peers, without the interference, regulation, manipulation and corruption of the financial system as we know it.

SATOCHI NAKAMOTO

That name is so far a legend in the undergrounds of geek world, but becoming really fast a recognized one on social stream :

No one knows for sure who Satochi Nakamoto is, or if is even the name of a real person, or maybe it is a group of people, but the simplicity of the story is this: he is a Japanese programmer, nobody knows for sure, that wrote and published in 2009, the white paper* of Bitcoin and the novel concept of cryptocurrency(*2) was born.

* *"A white paper is an authoritative document intended to fully inform the reader on a particular topic. It combines expert knowledge and research into a document that argues for a specific solution or recommendation. The white paper allows the reader to understand an issue, solve a problem, or make a decision. "* source: Wikipedia

(*2)cryptocurrency : A cryptocurrency (or crypto currency) is a digital asset designed to work as a medium of exchange wherein individual coin ownership records are stored in a digital ledger or computerized database using strong cryptography to secure transaction record entries, to control the creation of additional digital coin records, and to verify the transfer of coin ownership.[1] [2] It typically does not exist in physical form (like paper money) and is typically not issued by a central authority. Source Wikipedia

Truth is Satochi Nakamoto was not even the creator of the concept itself, it had been around ever since the internet was created, in 1993.

WHAT IS BITCOIN?

*Bitcoin is based on blockchain technology(*3).*

Blockchain(*3)a system in which a record of transactions made in bitcoin or another cryptocurrency are maintained across several computers that are linked in a peer-to-peer network.

"we can actually have a look at the blockchain and see evidence of what's going on"

— OXFORD DICTIONARY

A **blockchain**, originally block chain, **is** a growing list of records, called blocks, that are linked using cryptography. Wikipedia.com

I will give an example by comparison: If I go to the store, do my shopping and to pay for it, I pass my card through the card reader, The reader, connects my card data to the bank holding my savings and then the bank AUTHORIZES the transaction, the bank has the last word on it, not only to ok the transaction but, to change the records, to whoever harm or benefit that might effect, refuse to ok the transaction or make my assets disappear, even increase them, as they are only registered on their database.

You may be familiar with the process of issuing of the funds for the Stimulus/Bailout programs 2020, but in essence it was just a few strokes on a keyboard.

On the blockchain what happens is: Joe sends .005 of bitcoin(BTC) to Sam, the transaction is recorded at the same time on the whole of the network, that is; the same single operation is recorded in terminals around the globe and that record CANNOT be altered nor reversed.

There is not intervention from Central banks, Governments Etc.

It is only a business between Joe and Sam.

NEXT QUESTION IS: THEN WHAT OR WHO BACKS UP BITCOIN?

Bitcoin was born as one of the answers to the ultimate Libertarian-Anarchist dream: Small government size and no intervention in your money affairs.

No interference and corruption of the banking system in your personal financial decisions. Ideally it was an effort to getting off the control grid the establishment has set us in.

Part of this ideal was looked at as heaven for privacy just because transactions are private but not anonymous, contrary to public belief.

If you know what you are doing the transactions can be tracked to wallets (*4) and those wallet transactions are linked to IPs (your server/machine ID).

WALLETS

A cryptocurrency wallet is an app that allows cryptocurrency users to store and retrieve their digital assets. As with conventional currency, you don't need a wallet to spend your cash, but it certainly helps to keep it all in one place. When a user acquires cryptocurrency, such as bitcoins, he can store it in a cryptocurrency wallet and from there use it to make transactions.

So, who or what backs up Bitcoin? Short answer is No One, Bitcoin does not represent an asset, nor product, nor commodity.

Bitcoin has come a long way, the actual first bitcoin transaction is dated in 22 May 2010, by Laszlo Hanyecz, bought 2 pizzas for 10000 bitcoins in Jacksonville Fl.

An amount that would be nearly $99,950,000.00 if held in May 2020.

The email exchange of this pizza transaction is at the end of the chapter.

Yes, One BTC was worth some.07 cents back then and it is worth almost $10,000.00 dlls as of May 2020.

So what backs bitcoin? Nothing but certainty, from the public that it is going to be accepted as a means of exchange, from the merchants that offer goods and accept bitcoin as payment, and finally from speculators of about the same nature than those that speculate on stocks.

On that bitcoin has peaked at nearly $20K (Dec 2017) and it's volatility has "crushed it to the point of having "experts" to call for the bubble burst as many as 379 times" (Bitcoin obituary page/Bitcoin.com).

Consider this, there is only going to be 21,000,000 bitcoin total to be mined and 18.5 million have been mined.

Through a process that is called mining (servers handling Very complex problems getting rewarded with BTC).

The reward has gone from 50 btc daily at the beginning of 2010 for Miners, to 25 BTC daily after may 2012, to 12 btc daily after 2016 that process is called halving and it is detailed in the white paper. Next halving is expected in May 2020.

Since, mining has become a very expensive, energy wasting operation that requires bigger processors in larger numbers.

How long can it go?

Only to 21 Million unless radical changes are made.

Present scene for crypto is: Bitcoin is the first and oldest of the cryptocurrency. The crypto coinmarket cap(volume) is worth in May 2020 271+ billion (US dollars) and at its peak at the beginning of 2018 it reached almost half a Trillion, https://coinmarketcap.com/currencies.

This list above has more than 1400 coins, although the really strong players are not more than 100, as comparison the US stock market cap is worth 21 trillion Dollars. Data from data.com

What does this mean?

Crypto has reached just a small percentage of the market, less than 1%, and the bitcoin is now worth 10K each. As the curve of acceptation of crypto grows the market cap will grow and from there we just get into more of Bitcoin as an expanding investment tool.

Had you invested in 2010, as much as $100.00 in Bitcoin (BTC) you would be at almost $4 Million in the profit in June 2013 and it would be almost $12,500,000 in May 2020.

It has crashed a few times though, always to rise to new levels, go figure.

It is said that the utility of Bitcoin is storage of value, in a nut shell that is what it is.

Other coins have embraced new development of the blockchain technology and their uses have expanded to an ample scope of uses, and that may help to speed up the adoption of this type of currency by the public.

Today's world is moving on in terms of digital tech advances, many countries and central banks are considering issue of digital central currencies, that is a whole different subject, not for this book.

And this writing should in no shape or form, be constructed as financial advice, your forecast should be a result of your research and the quality of that research will give you a number you can think with but consider this:

"Never invest more resources than you are willing to risk."

INVESTMENT OPPORTUNITIES

That is history above, what is actually happening is this: A new technology is still in its early stages of acceptance, and those few that have already embraced it are enjoying an amazing position, the first few on the line.

Here are some examples, LM a young entrepreneur from the Southwest, started buying and trading bitcoin really early back in Dec. 2011, being a bank analyst, he bought his first 100 dollars in BTC, because maybe there was something on it, @ 2.00 dollars a piece, 50 bitcoins, then actually started trading it in 2013 when BTC was trading for $102.00

He then started mining, which is basically having a computer set to participate on the solving of VERY complex Math problems on the BTC network, odds of solving some are 1 in 13 trillion; then starting his own mining operation around 2014. Mind you BTC cost was then $340 and last data I have on that, he had about 800 machines mining in 2 separate locations in the US.

He then went onto building a platform that basically participates in the first spinoff of this market: Gaming, and the industry of over 93 billion dollars a year.

He has already created his own coin (his company has) to facilitate his customers transactions while gaming.

You may be like I was, having a short opinion of all these kids that seem to be wasting their lives away, sitting in front of a computer gaming, well, I don't sit on fixed opinions about things, a kid of a close friend was making more money at 12 years old than his oldest brother at age 17, how?

Gaming, and getting paid for gaming on this crypto thingy and cashing out about 3-400 dollars a month, that was back in 2016. Have you ever heard of Twitch? Maybe you should, not all kids make money this way but if your kid plays and expends day after day on this activity, he could use some guidance.

The volatility of the crypto market is appealing and scary at the same time; to give you an example a coin that is not even among the first 20 on the coin market cap, MATIC went from 0.00000237 a piece (aprox 2 cents of a dollar) to.00000304(

aprox 3 cents a piece) on a 6:30 hrs period to crash back down to .00000257 next day, not for the light hearted but what's the reason for the hard core crypto fans all in this.

How come?

First it is not a regulated market, the way stock market and Forex are, sort of a libertarian spot, not totally anyways, but back up to 2017 when BTC hit his highest at $19950.00 approx. The market was like the wild west, where anything could and was happening.

Another acquaintance story I would like to tell you, JS started to learn about crypto in 2016, in learning along the way he put in $1000.00 and started his trading career, not really familiar with the details but his first year he made over $40,000.00 dollars.

Now the purpose of those stories is not to create the idea that crypto is the easiest market to make money, it is not, it can be made if you are willing to learn and enthusiastic about the possibilities of this market and aware of the risks, as well as the scams that have been abundant on this.

Another story, a friend of a friend bought 2 BTC in March 2018 at around 7K a piece, price then went down to 3K, during these past 2 years, he could have recovered his investment, if he cashed out at any of the peaks that the price has reached since, he has not so far and in any case it was money he was prepared to lose.

There is another Crypto field that has not bloomed as it should. I am talking about ICO's (initial crypto offering) equivalent of IPO's. Many new digital companies since back in 2010s were looking at this new form of fund raising, it is made by a company that develops a project and then organizes a form of crowd sales by offering of crypto currency, issued by the same company, in short that is an ICO, these coins usually come attached to a token which means there is a digital contract issued on each coin, that gives the buyer a certain amount of coins(being the regular investment $100.00 back then) that will give you, as a holder of tokens, you have some rights to the possible future benefits on the company, it is a form to facilitate the company's access to resources to fund speeding up their research and applications of blockchain tech,.

Giving access to small investors, the possibility to build a portfolio before the tokens would hit the market. So you would support the company, almost as if you were a shareholder in it, the added benefit would be that if the project goes right the ROI is quite impressive, but this is also a really speculative approach and must be regarded as that and proceed cautiously.

Much needed regulation came about in the ICO field when one too many spoiled apples threatened to spoil the rest, meaning a few fake ICO scams and finally it looked like some order was introduced by regulators when they (ICO's) were defined as securities middle of 2018 by the SEC (US Securities and

Exchange Commission,) however no other motion has been made to push forward regulations.

Here are some examples of what those ICO's have helped build:

- Neo: original price of token was 0.032 cents, its highest price has been $162.11, it's current price 1$0.80.
- Monsterbyte: gambling platform ICOs, on July 2017 sold out in 5 minutes and was valued at .11 cents per token
- Kik messaging app raised $100 million on it's ICO
- Those are just a few of the many success stories.

The personal successes that I know of are from 2017, many say those days are gone, however here is something to think about.

D.H. had been into ICOs for 2 years basically searching for good, solid projects, would buy tokens wait for the release of the currency and sell one. Of the successes was Game Pro, a project related to gaming and a sharing platform, DH invested $1000.00, she made 60K on the first 2 weeks.

DIGITAL MONEY AND CRYPTO CURRENCY: CHANGE

We are at the dawn of digital applied technologies, artificial intelligence and robotics. There are white hats and we have black hats, the race is on in terms of what country will reach supremacy in the next couple of decades, maybe less.

What we are taking a long time to realize is that life as we know it, is changing; shopping, banking, manufacturing, transportation, entertainment and communications are some of the industries where these changes are more obvious, but as a society, we are headed to new times. Crypto started as an effort to keep control mechanisms out of the hands of governments and large corporations, and preserve your privacy so you would have a reasonable chance to profit from those changes, however it would be silly to imagine that those agents mentioned above are not going to take advantage of these technologies.

We see the Govt. development of central digital currencies, as the Venezuelan Petro or the Russian digital Ruble or the most recent Chinese e-Yuan, even the US with the digital Dollar, are efforts to tighten up the control factor over your wallet and the way you spend your money. China with it's progress on face recognition technology and it's mostly successful attempts to keep it's own citizens out of the internet as we know it, and it's infamous social credit system, are all just hints of what choices we are facing in regard of AI, Automatization and Crypto technologies.change.

CRYPTO MARKET CAP

How large is the crypto market nowadays? This would be the total value of all coins (amount of coins multiplied by its price). As of today 277+ billion dollars, with about 60+billion exchanged in any given day, but as high as that may look, it's not really as impressive as the stock market shares that just in the US is worth 43 trillion dollars.

What that tells us has two viewpoints:

One, there is not yet a high degree of acceptability by the investment institutions of the viability and sustainability of the crypto universe, as a whole. We have a large number of organizations that use the blockchain technology in increasing numbers, but just don't have the big investors to trust completely to go large on crypto as an exchange of value.

Second, and in an optimistic way, the percentage of the money market that knows or uses crypto as money is really tiny, if in any given moment the acceptance of crypto or bitcoin more specifically goes to even 2% of the market we may see a great increase in the price of the Bitcoin, that is a highly speculative view but it tells you some of what is keeping the Bitcoin being a bigger thing.

IS THERE ANY OTHER TYPE OF CRYPTO BESIDES BITCOIN?

There are around 1700 coins in the coin market cap, but not all of them have a major use, most traders would place their bets on the top 20 with some taking bets on some of the most interesting coins and projects on the top 100 to trade.

To introduce you to different technologies akin to the crypto concept of Blockchain forms, here are some others.

ETHEREUM

It also uses blockchain technology as bitcoin does, but there is blockchain and there is Ethereum blockchain technology, let me explain.

The blockchain bitcoin is based on was designed to make pair to pair transactions possible, pretty simple and straightforward. Ethereum's blockchain however, represents a huge improvement on scalability compared with that of bitcoin, it is an open source platform that has the capability of building in and enabling smart contracts, time machines and distributed applications to be built and run without any fraud, control, interference or downtime from a third party. Capabilities bitcoin does not have.

Ethereum was built as the next blockchain generation to increase appeal on use and adoption of this technology.

Ethereum is the second coin in the crypto market cap and it is a platform which is used for several other projects to build on their own applications and smart contracts, which escalate the capabilities of blockchain for different uses, privacy, reduced costs of transfers (a big stop on Bitcoin acceptability by the market), connection with third-party providers of value add services, are some of the advantages introduced by those projects using Ethereum blockchain technology. It was introduced by Vitalik Buterin.

Why has it not displaced Bitcoin? Bitcoin has some characteristics that have been proved valuable for the users of crypto, though it has a limited set amount of coins shorter than Ethereum, it is also easier to liquidate compared to Ethereum.

Another important factor is; Once Bitcoin boomed back in 2017, a huge setback was observed; the cost of transactions was becoming prohibitive. To give you an example; during an event for the crypto community in LA an assistant won a prize, a modest one. She answered a question and she won a cup of coffee worth of bitcoin, something on the order of 7 or 8 dollars, problem was that on transfer of the bitcoin the cost was around $12.00.

The point that was being made was: the cost was increasingly becoming a problem, we got the point.

The possibility of adoption by the real consumers was pretty much in peril. Not to mention the time that would take for some of these transfers to get through was sometimes about a 3 hours wait, it would be ridiculous in the real service trade scene.

Then in 2018 the solution came to view, Bitcoin lighting network(BLN), a revolution on the Crypto universe to make the cost of transfers and time of them to be real competitive.

You can check what BLN is in Wikipedia, but to make it short, it is payment protocol that solves the bitcoin scalability problem.

Ethereum has not run with the same ingenuity by its developers. To make a transfer possible in the Ethereum network, one uses "gas", which refers to the cost necessary to make a transaction on the network, miners set the price of gas and once the price has been set, the transaction can be declined if that threshold is not met.

Then at a certain point in 2018, when Ethereum price reached $1400.00, it presented a prohibitive increase in cost of gas, that factor in itself has prevented Ethereum from taking over Bitcoin as the king of crypto. Absurd? Yes, has it been solved? Not just yet. Although that impasse has been approached successfully by some other projects that use the Ethereum blockchain to build their own blockchain and have resolved cost-time difficulty.

You may want to check them out, Omisego, Vet, Dash, Cardano among others with some of them showing really interesting features like scalability, security, speed and anonymity, some have them all, some have few of them, do your due diligence before investing.

So you see Bitcoin was able to handle the setback and Ethereum has not yet done so.

Still Ethereum is very strong, it has crypto market confidence and that is a valued asset.

Now in terms of value, as in "how can make this money for me?"

When Ethereum was first created and released to the market, July 2015, it had a low point of.42 Cents in OCT 2015 up to $1432.00 at certain point somewhere at the beginning of 2018, and today $382.90 as of August 2nd 2020.

Why the volatility you ask? Remember, Crypto is a market that has not been regulated yet, at least not completely, although some initiatives have been taken, around the globe, some of them going so far as banning the whole of the exchange or some of the related activities, like mining, stocking etc. but some have been more logical like applying NYC banking regulations to those platforms that sell Bitcoin. As of February 2020 Bitcoin is legal in USA, Japan, Canada, The UK and most developed countries. In the US you should check the SEC/IRS guidelines for taxpayers on crypto.

IS THIS MARKET RISKY?

The short answer is, yes. Remember, as always in investing, do your own research, but nevertheless with a bullish prediction on the middle term, it keeps being attractive to the crypto universe fans.

With that said, what about: Where do I keep my crypto if I have it?

Security is a must in regard of money and assets, and crypto has an inherent characteristic that needs to be addressed.

You will never set your hands on it, you will never see it physically, it is the natural born son of the internet, a totally digital recorded mark on some digital ledger on the cloud.

How do you keep it safe?

WALLETS

With Crypto, no bank keeps your assets, savings, trades nor investments in storage, that is the nature of this, remember? It is supposed to be decentralized. So how do we do it ourselves?

Electronic wallets exist so you can safely keep your crypto away from thieves, hackers and the sort. How effective and secure are they, lets find out.

THERE ARE 2 TYPES OF WALLETS:

Hot wallet: Basically, any wallet sitting online is considered to be hot, whether you keep your Bitcoin at an exchange while you trade, or keep it in your own app such as Blockchainwalletapp, they are still "hot wallets", the difference is that in your own wallets you create what is call "keys", and you can safeguard those keys offline so more or less keep your Bitcoin or Ethereum etc. safe.

In the case of an exchange site like Coinbase, Binance, Bitrex etc, you create the keys and some other safeguard measures but Bitcoin is kept connected to the internet (so to speak) to make trades, most of traders would keep a minimal amount in their exchange wallets and safely off line the rest.

There have been some memorable hacks that have shook the crypto world, NiceHash in 2017 (cloud mining) the company has repaid their users so far 81% of the stolen bitcoin...

Bitpoint in July 2017 (exchange) investigations are still on going.

Bitrex in May 2018 (exchange) although in this case it was the project itself.

Bitgold the one hacked not the exchange, the project has repaid 255000 BTG coins so far.

And the infamous Mt Gox the largest exchange company in 2013, suffered 2 strong attacks, one on 2011 and the second in a number of years

during 2012-2014, 850,000 BTC stolen, although 200,000 have been recovered but are yet to be returned to users.

If you want more details on these cases go to cointelegraph>news>crypto.

It is an interesting read if you are into crypto.

But again those were the times with Zero regulations, security recommendations like two factor authentifications, NYC, email verification or IP tracking were not in place.

We have moved a ways from that. More regulation/security is possible.

Cold wallet- is a hardware device, its name means cold storage, you transfer your crypto to the wallet and disconnect the device from the internet and as long as you don't lose it (the same way you wouldn't lose your physical cash wallet) and keep safe your private keys, you are safe.

Ledger Nano (@ $119), Trezor are some of the best known cold wallets. Is hacking possible on these? The possibilities always exist, given that most of the hacking happens due to social engineering, meaning not because someone connects to your device but because you trust somebody with your private keys, and this is the same as if you have a key to a banking vault, you lose the key and you lose the assets.

2020 AND CRYPTO

These are interesting times, challenging and full of questions, but less answers.

Bitcoins main feature was supposed to be a storage of wealth and it is still the flagship of crypto, with at least 60% of the capital in the coin market cap and at this point 117 billion dollars of capitalization. With an increase of value for the last few months, March to August 2020 that represent a gain of 290% - it has not delivered as yet.

For the very first time in many generations the world has come to a standstill (2020) and for some it could have been the break point for Bitcoin to assert itself as what it was announced, though traditional investors have not seen it that way. And it is running out of time.

What does that mean? Graphs don't show it increasing its value since it's peak in 2017, it's wearing off. It is not being adopted in mass, it is not preferred over Gold (which was one of the more daring comparisons made by experts).

Does it mean Crypto is doomed? No of course not, it only means that the technological breakthrough that Bitcoin presented has been improved by other projects, that the more diverse features of other projects are becoming more attractive for users other than just crypto enthusiasts.

Automatization, Artificial intelligence, robotics have disrupted the way we used to plan life just a few years ago, Blockchain offers new potential uses

that those sold on Bitcoin blockchain were only dreaming just 10 years ago.

Will Bitcoin vanish? Maybe. Can it be improved to keep it up to date? Hardly, without risking changing it into something else. And in the end it really does not matter, because Bitcoin is not an end in itself, ever since the first few people were looking at how to release the grip that the financial system has over society, it was conceived as a tool, and it has, as such opened many patterns to follow.

And this writing should in no way, shape or form, be constructed as a financial forecast. Your forecast should be a result of your research and the quality of that research will give you a number you can think with but consider this:

"Never invest more resources than you are willing to risk completely losing."

TAKEAWAY FROM THIS CHAPTER:

crypto is a good alternative/safe guard to the central banking systems. It's here to stay and I consider it similar to but lesser in value to Gold and Silver.

BCL

10

PENSIONS

What did I always hear from my parents? "Get a good job with a pension and you will be ok. Government or city jobs have that ".

So I did apply, to be an LAPD policeman and a city of LA worker. Thank goodness, those never went thru, being a police in LA right now, no thank you (riots,curfews). Hey, 20 years isn't so long to wait. My dad has a pension with IBM after 28 years service to them in two different states.

This chapter I will quote a lot from the Book by Robert Kyosaki and Edward Siedle *"Who Stole My Pension?"* It's a good read.

First the book above is written in a very unusual format for two authors.

Every chapter has a DB section and then a DC section.

Let me explain. DB pensions are (defined benefits). Edward handles this, covering all Pensions that are State, City or Federal pensions and Public works.

The DC Pensions are (defined contributions). Private pensions such as 401k,

IRA, SEP etc and RRSPs, etc(Registered Retirement Savings Plan) Canadian Govt. version of 401k. 401K can be both DB – DC in some ways.

The amount of shadow banking going on with these pensions is HUGE.

Especially the DB side of pensions.

SHADOW BANKING

Shadow banking is complex, and most would think it would be the financial derivatives, mortgage backed securities (MBS) credit default swaps (CDS) etc that most of us knew nothing about until Lehman Bros collapsed or were kept hidden from us INTENTIONALLY.

But really, *it is **all** the unregulated off-balance sheet dealings and transactions that are going on with such as SIVs,(Special Investment Vehicles,see glossary) and many are sold and resold to these State and Local pensions AS INVESTMENTS.*

3 main things occurred before "shadow banking" came into effect in the 1980's.

One, 1971 Nixon took the Dollar off the Gold standard, allowing huge debt to start.

Two, 1987 Allan Greenspan Fed Reserve Bank Chairman, bails out Wall street after the 1987 stock market crash.

Three, The 1999 Bill Clinton POTUS Repeal of the Glass-Steagall ACT which separated investment banking from retail banking. The repeal in 1999 then allowed deposited money in retail banks to be invested into financial derivatives such as MBS etc.

SUBPRIME MORTAGES WAS A MAIN APPARENT CAUSE OF THE 2008 BUBBLE BURST.

In 2020, There is such a thing as SUBPRIME PENSIONS.

The amount of underfunded Pensions in the US is huge.

To list a few DB State by state.

The most funded DB State Pensions are as of 2018 July 19 The Wall Street Journal reports:

1. South Dakota 100% funded
2. Wisconsin 99.9% funded
3. Washington 98.7% funded

The Worst funded in the 50 states:

48. Connecticut 51.9% funded
49. Kentucky 48.9% funded
50. Illinois 47.1% funded

17 other States have Pensions less than two thirds funded.

A LOT of Pensions are invested in these "Shadow Banking" products.

They are sold and resold to other Pensions as MBS, and many other three letter "products" or derivatives.

THE GOVERNMENT, WHERE ARE THEY IN THIS?

You are probably thinking," The Government would not let them rip us off, they will protect us, somebody does care in the Govt. "You are right, some do care.

There is the PBGC (Pension Benefit Guarantee Corp.) This is the Federal agency created by ERISA(Employment Retirement Income Security Act) to protect and Insure private DB pensions. If your company went bankrupt, PBGC is the institution that would oversee your Pension dollars or payments.

The 1974 ERISA, is not an ACT to look after public Pensions, but all others, such as IBM, Intel, HP, John Deere, Bayer, Eli Lilly, United Airlines etc.

Bankruptcy proceedings can seriously cut and unfund Billions in owed Pension benefits. Witness the great City of Detroit, filed bankruptcy 2013, the proceedings let the City out of 12 Billion in payments and healthcare obligations owed to its workers. The Biggest Municipality bankruptcy in US history.

To quote Ed Siedle from "Who Stole My Pension ?"

"While PGBC publicly states its mission is to ensure that corporations sponsoring defined benefit Pensions are prepared to honor their obligations to workers, its private agenda is to assist corporations in abandoning their pension obligations. The US Govt.'s belief is that if American corporations are to compete globally in the future, they must be freed from promises they made to their employees over the past 60 years or so."

Strong words from a strong, highly experienced pension Authority and former SEC Attorney, Edward Siedle.

With ERISA, one mandate of it is responsible for conducting an annual Audit of all non State, Local and Federal Pensions.

But in fact, about only 40% of corporate Pensions actually get audited.

Your Pension may *never* have been properly audited.

2011 From Inspector General DOL (US DEPARTMENT OF LABOR) On limited scope "no opinion" audits, "These "no opinion" Audits provide no substantive assurance of asset integrity to plan participants or the Department"

Not good news, but I will show you something to do if you are in this Pension mess at the end of this chapter.

UNDERFUNDED?

This word basically means the Pension has promised to pay more money than it has in it.

If you can get a copy of your Pensions Annual report summary look under the "funding ratio" of the report. This number is a ratio of Assets to Liabilities. If the ratio is over 100 it is overfunded. If the ratio is below 100 it is Underfunded. If it well below 100, you better contact your Union representative or the Plan administrator and get some answers.

WHAT WOULD WARREN BUFFET RECOMMEND?

Well he is the 3rd richest guy in America at 90 Billion. You might want to listen to his advice on investing.

As Edward Seidle said in "Who stole my Pension"

"What are Pensions doing globally ? The exact opposite of what Warren Buffet told them to do- with predictably disastrous results"

BY:

"Using overly optimistic investment return assumptions Gambling in high-cost high-risk hedge and private equity investments Paying exponentially greater "obscene" fees to Wall Street Entrusting assets to firms Buffet regards as dishonest Eschewing the lowest cost passively managed investments Moving further and further from transparency "

WHAT CAN I DO ABOUT IT ?

You and your fellow pensioners can get together and crowdfund a Forensic Investigation of your pension by a pension expert. This will be transparency, unbiased. Use the internet to gain all the connections to your possible thousands of workers and assemble.

There is power in numbers. There may be FORMIDABLE opposition from the Pension overseers. Persist on.

In May 2015, in 29 days of crowdfunding, 349 backers/pensioners contributed just over $20K to investigate the Rhode Island State fund. The first ever.

If you happen to be in California in the CALPERS public Pension, there is approx 1.7 million members and the Pension is at about 70% funded at Jan 2020, so you will need a larger more experienced firm like Ed Siedle and staff and more money to hire them, near 750k.

Be sure to define with the investigator the parameters such as scope and length of the investigation and that you will be able to publicize the findings for federal and state bodies to see.

TAKEAWAY FROM THIS CHAPTER: MAKE YOUR OWN PENSION.

And if you already have one with a company, take care of it, legally. Get Persistent as F*ck, if needed.

BCL

11

LIFE

In life it starts with you. And my number **one** investment, before Gold, Real Estate, Stocks etc, is ME. If I am in bad shape and unproductive, how much can I help anything or anyone?

By that I mean, I can take with me only so much when I leave, I can take the abilities I have, (possibly there are more than you think.)

I can take the knowledge I have and will still get. There is a lot to know.

I study daily.

I can take my own condition regarding everything else: did I help my family, my groups, mankind, the animal world, the physical world, the spiritual world and lastly, god. ?

If I choose to come back to this, what am I coming back to ? It can be good or bad. I cannot read the distant future.

Well, life. No matter what happens, you are going to live thru it.

> "I'm not afraid of death because I don't believe in it. It's just getting out of one car, and into another."
>
> — JOHN LENNON

There's going to be winners, there's going to be losers, and there's going to be people that seem to change very little, but one thing's for sure change will happen and hopefully for the good. Nothing stays the same.

But in May 2020 here it's been a little rough in the USA, people are wondering will I go back to work? Will the Dodgers play again? Will I be able to go out and exercise? Can we go to church ? Will I find work again?

I don't know when you're going to read this book but it's been that bad, our Constitutional rights infringed upon.(no right to go to church for months, must wear a face mask, stopping travel, no right to assemble and businesses shut down.) Infringed upon, No Doubt.

"It's easier to fool people than to convince them they have been fooled"

— AMERICAN AUTHOR, MARK TWAIN

Unfortunately, this Twain quote is very apropos for this chapter and these times, if you asked me this Covid 19 was a BIGG fool, influenza has a vaccine for decades and still kills way more people than Covid 19 ever did. Did we shut down the world for INFLUENZA ? NO and you never should. A big overreaction at minimum this Covid 19.

With a lot of more destruction/shutdown than help, the Govt. control created wayyy more harm than good, a LIABILITY for sure. Especially here in California.

I'm no conspiracy theorist here, but this shutdown event was unprecedented harm. In my opinion, testing us to see how far we could be pushed.

SURVIVAL

May 2020, Now these are times when I start thinking, *"wow, maybe I should have a gun ? Maybe I should have more gold and silver for insurance? Maybe I should stockpile food. What do I need to be, do and have to Survive?"*

These questions are not out of left field, or are not irrational thoughts because things can get worse than they are. Worst case scenario.

Well, I have watched a lot of Survivorman Show with Les Stroud, but he only does 7 days in the wild without supplies. I love Les and we can learn a lot from him but, we need to think with more than 7 days. 6 months would be nice. The more the merrier.

And in the words of the money mentor

Robert Kiyosaki, from his book FAKE.FAKE MONEY, FAKE TEACHERS, FAKE ASSETS.

"to be a realist it is important to be both a pessimist and an optimist. I am optimistic about the future. I'm also a pessimist about the future being a pessimist I prepare for the future with the five G's, they are:

1. *Gold and Silver*
2. *Grub: food for at least 6 months*

3. *Gasoline*
4. *Ground: I have safe properties with food and water away from cities.*
5. *Guns and Ammo: both guns and ammo serve as protection and currency."*

I know all of you cannot necessarily afford all this listed here, but you can do some of it and be prepared for whatever, Coronavirus or whatever virus, war etc.

These may seem extreme but, I like to look at the worst case scenario in life, investing and in business to gauge its potential and know some limits.

Example: you get married and the she empties your bank account and sleeps with your friend. I'm ok, I dump her and find a better woman as I KNOW WHAT I DID WRONG and take full responsibility for the scene. (Also, I have other bank accounts.)

Example: your 12 unit apartment building is at half capacity due to move out and non payers (Covid 19 style), but you can still make the mortgage payment and break even, due to your proper planning, equity and not being overleveraged.

Example: I loan someone money for an investment where I'm supposed to get 30% plus my capital back. He loses the money due to the Covid 19 quarantine shutdown. But I can afford to lose the money as, *I never loan or invest money I feel I could not live without.*

With this viewpoint I can have a baseline from where I or the company/investment can be at worst and how far it is from viable.

If I see a worst-case/very bad scenario and it's not too far from that viability point, I know it's a good investment or it can be a good business, if even in it's worst case scenario, it's still alive and flowing cash it may be near viable.

Viability point would be where the business or investment is making money(profit) and not a liability.

YOU. YOUR SURVIVAL.

In your life you may need to move, literally change where you live, I have personally lived in Florida, Arizona, California (LA and San Jose), and Virginia. After 52 years in a few cities, I have a pretty good sense of where the money is, and exceptional people. Of course, I do find good people everywhere.

You may need to move to where the money or opportunity **is.** It may not be in Keokuk, Iowa for you.

Real estate is not the same opportunity in Israel and other places as it is here in the USA.

In my life at the age of 16 I was forced into Desert Hills boys school in Tucson AZ, not fun, but it was a right action in that it separated me from some suppressive influences, (drugs, criminals) and forced me to dry out and study while not under the influence of drugs and have a daily regimen. It was a BIG change for me. Believe me at first, I could NOT see how it would help me. I was *very* different from what I am today.

I have seen my son who started on the dark path of drugs and crime, like I was as a teenager. But then one of the ways I helped him was by getting him out of the environment, Los Angeles into a different area and people, Tucson, AZ. This helped him, even though Tucson is a slightly criminal area, it is better than LA.

So about 18 months later, while in Tucson he asked for help and we got him into a drug rehab situation, in Kansas City, where he is doing well and living a very productive life at 22 y/o.

There's a lot to be said for moving and a change of environment. It can help in ways you probably never thought of.

One of my jobs as a parent is to teach the child, how to stand on their own

and not need bailouts or parents and to be able to possibly take care of me one day.

Knowing what works with money and life can go a long way to helping them survive well.

And that is the BIGGEST understatement in this book.

PEOPLE.

"You can tell more about a person by what he says about others than you can by what others say about him."

— AUDREY HEPBURN - ACTRESS (1929 - 1993)

This is crucial. The right people and how to pick them. Most do not really know how.

The right wife, the proper sales manager, your high havingness treasury person. Where are they? Who can you trust?

Well I'm not going to tell you how either, but I can tell you if you email me, I will refer you to an online course that is FREE on it.

I have done this course and I would say it has saved my life, by knowing what to look for in PEOPLE.

I have learned the hard way on this, and even when you can't pick them, there is some way to be cause in the situation, no matter what.

Choosing the right people can literally save your life too, much less your business or an investment.

BCL

CONCLUSION

Well I hope you made it through to the end of the book safely here and not too upset to leave a nice review. Some of this book is hard to look at and could get some people emotional. It could also literally, *save a life.*

I do push things in people's faces occasionally and there's a few things in here that cover life and the world that some people definitely do not know or understand and *possibly* disagree with. I imagine a couple people that read this book **will disapprove/hate it**. I can't please everyone, but I can please most.

I promise you, if I didn't think it could help you, it wouldn't be in this book.

To restate some of the Main points/tools of this book, in the order given.

1. Policy
2. Disconnecting, hostile customers
3. Sub Products
4. Decision Making
5. Drilling
6. Online reviews Yelp Etc
7. Mindset to Succeed
8. Failure
9. Banking
10. LLC or Corporation
11. Workers Compensation
12. The Tax man/woman
13. Business loans
14. Liens
15. Appreciation
16. Real Estate
17. The Market
18. Leverage
19. Multi-Family
20. Property Value
21. The Wrong Tenant
22. Rent Control
23. "We buy your house for Cash"
24. Stocks, 401ks, Etfs, Bonds, REITS and Gold and Silver
25. College
26. Online Businesses
27. Employee

28. Youtube/Online Teachers
29. The Side Hustle
30. Amazon
31. Recession,Depressions,Covid 19
32. Acceptance
33. Pretend you got nothing.
34. Liabilities that were assets. and Vice Versa.
35. Perfectionism
36. Spending, your life and business.
37. Discipline. Spending
38. Sales In Business and Life.
39. CRM
40. Mail!
41. The Sale
42. The Close
43. Sales in Life & Investing
44. Men and Women, Sales.
45. Sales Follow-Up
46. Sales Believe in your Product
47. Sales Rules
48. Govt Pgms SBA PPP UI EIDL
49. EDD
50. What happened in 2008?
51. Bailouts.
52. Cryptocurrency
53. HOT Wallet
54. Crypto, Change

55. Pensions
56. Shadow Banking
57. Where is the Govt. in this?
58. Underfunded?
59. What can I do about this?
60. Life
61. Survival
62. You. Your Survival.
63. People
64. Conclusion
65. The Government
66. Brett Lemos

I missed a few in the list but that's a lot of tools and data to get you going on a workable path, succeeding in Life and not losing money.

Put them into practice, being the person who has Big Goals, has money, is successful and happy.

Doing the things that accomplish the Big Goals, making the sales, getting the property, making your team.

Then have it, have the good, the bad and the Journey.

A life without some Journey, sounds done to me.

Always have something to look forward to, then Persist like F*ck to get it.

THE US GOVERNMENT

> "And this I must fight against: any idea, religion, or government which limits or destroys the individual."
>
> — JOHN STEINBECK - WRITER (1902 - 1968)

You might get the idea as you went through this book that I don't trust the US government, and you'd be right in thinking that.

For all I know Social Security may not even be there for me or us (I will be 65 in 2033), but I hope I never have to take dollar one from Social Security and I hope that my own efforts here act as help for you to be able to make more of your life, now *and never need* SS, UI etc. money also.

I like POTUS Donald Trump, he's a winner and knows business, I believe he has all the money he ever needs and doesn't need to be shady and receive kickbacks etc.

At the same time, it doesn't matter who is POTUS, you still got to go out there and hustle, sell it like you mean it and bring home the bacon.

Just like I do, even if some other Biden, or Clinton is elected, Nov 2020,

I'm out there hustling the next big thing for our company and our family.

Thinking BIG. Doing Big, Having Big.

No Matter who/what is in the Government.

BRETT LEMOS

Part of the reason that this book comes off in a way that you might like, is because I care.

I care about how it looks, how much it can help someone or not, and **how much truth is in it.**

I lead by example and people do copy you when you are successful.

This same type of caring is what I recommend to control your life, business and relations in a successful way as I have in mine. Professionals give focused attention to details the novice misses. Be a professional.

The main focus I had for this book was to help you, no matter what the world has or you have going on, to succeed in business, investing and in life.

And absolutely positively to not lose money, that's why I recommend what I recommend in this book.

> "Rule #1 never lose money. Rule #2, Don't forget rule #1"
>
> — WARREN BUFFET, CEO OF BERKSHIRE HATHAWAY

Reach me at BrettLemosL12@gmail.com

Two things I ask you to do now, one, leave a review on Amazon and two, use this data and do well.

Any questions, I will do my best to answer them personally.

Your Friend.

BCL

GLOSSARY

Apropos: fitting, suitable: relevant to the scene ballon payment: usually indicating a loan with smaller interest only payments until end of loan term which has a final, large outstanding principal payment.

Bargaining: is a line of defense against the emotions of **grief**. It helps you postpone the sadness, confusion, or hurt.

Resource https://www.healthline.com/health/stages-of-grief

CARES ACT: March 27 2020 Coronavirus Aid, Relief, and Economic Security Act

This law addressed the bailout of US citizens and businesses due to the Covid 19 crisis.

CDS: credit default swap, a form of credit default insurance sold to a security holder to protect default by someone like Lehman

Bros. In that case Sept 2008, Lehman holding too much MBS insured with CDS . The MBS were full of subprime(but labeled prime falsely) loans.

"It is even possible for investors to effectively switch sides on a credit default swap to which they are already a party. For example, if a CDS seller believes that the borrower is likely to default, the CDS seller can buy its own CDS from another institution or sell the contract to another bank in order to offset the risks. The chain of ownership of a CDS can become very long and convoluted, which makes tracking the size of this market difficult." investopedia.com/terms/c/creditdefaultswap.asp

Double talk: ambiguous or evasive communication.

Resource: American Heritage Dictionary 2nd College edition

DSM: Published by The American Psychiatric Association. The **Diagnostic and Statistical Manual** of Mental Disorders (DSM) is the book used by health care professionals in the U. S. and approx. half of the world as the Medical guide to diagnosis of mental disorders.

"The DSM contains descriptions, symptoms, values and other requirements for diagnosing mental disorders." Currently DSM 5 is the latest edition as of April 2020.

Resource https://www.psychiatry.org/psychiatrists/practice/dsm/feedback-and-questions/frequently-asked-questions

Edify: an improving influence on the mind. edification. Oxford School Dictionary

Equity: the residual value of a business or property beyond any mortgage, American Heritage Dictionary. In my words, the money/value left over after all debt is paid on a property.

ERISA:1974 Employee Retirement Security Act: Law enacted to protect private industry workers with the Minimum standards for pensions. One rule is the annual audit of all privatized Pensions be conducted. R.Kyosaki, R. Seidle, *Who stole my Pension?* Copyright 2020 Plata Publishing Scottsdale AZ

ETF : Exchange-traded fund

In the most basic sense, an **ETF** is a type of fund that owns assets — like stocks, commodities, or futures — but has its ownership divided into shares that trade on stock exchanges. In other words, investors can buy and sell **ETFs** whenever they want during trading hours.

Resource https://www.businessinsider.com/guide-to-how-etfs-work-2018-1

FDIC: The Federal Deposit Insurance Corporation (**FDIC**) is an independent federal agency insuring deposits in U.S. banks and savings and loans in the event of bank failure. The **FDIC** , created in 1933 to continue public confidence and promote stability in the financial system through promotion of sound banking practices.

Resource https://www.fdic.gov/about/learn/symbol/index.html five stages: denial, anger, bargaining, depression and **acceptance** are a part of the framework that makes up our learning to live with the one we lost. They are tools to help us frame and identify what we may be feeling. But they are not stops on some linear timeline in grief.

Resource https://grief.com/the-five-stages-of-grief/

fund: is a group of capital belonging to numerous investors used to collectively purchase securities while each investor keeps ownership and guidance of his own shares.

Glass-Steagall Act of 1933: The **Glass-Steagall Act** is a 1933 law that separated investment banking from retail banking. Investment banks/institutions organized the initial sales of stocks, called an IPO (initial public offering). They facilitated mergers and acquisitions. Repeal would be to take it out of law/effect. This repeal of Glass- Steagall in 1999 allowed banks to invest deposited funds into financial derivatives like MBS. (see MBS in glossary)

Gulp: comment of fear or uncertainty, a swallowing sound in throat.

Hedge Fund: large investment portfolios including anything, metals, real estate, stocks, bonds, DERIVATIVES etc. These are available only to accredited investors, usually requiring large minimum investments.

Inundation: receiving so much you cannot deal with it; overwhelm.

K1 Schedule : this is the IRS form that itemizes your depreciation, earnings, credits and losses for investment Rental properties/ including also SFR for investment .

Leverage: in real estate is using borrowed money to buy a property.

Resource https://www.fool.com/millionacres/real-estate-basics/real-estate-terms/what-leverage-real-estate-and-how-do-you-use-it/

Market Cap : This would be the total value of all coins ,shares etc.(amount of coins multiplied by its price).

PBGC: Pension Benefit Guarantee Corporation

"PBGC is a federal agency created by the Employee Retirement Income Security Act of 1974 (ERISA) to protect pension benefits in private-sector defined benefit plans - the kind that typically pay a set monthly amount at retirement. ... Your plan is insured even if your employer fails to pay the required premiums." Resource www.PBGC.gov

POTUS: President of the United States.

prospectus: is a formal document that is required by and filed with the Securities and Exchange Commission (SEC) that provides details about an investment offering to the public. Resource www.investopedia.com

REIT: a real estate investment trust. This is where you own shares of an entity (a Corporation or LLC) that owns real estate. You are not a partner. You do not get schedule K1 depreciation (see K1 above) to deduct on your taxes. You usually get paid dividends every 3 months .

RULE of 72: The **Rule of 72** is a quick, useful formula that is popularly used to estimate the number of years required to double the invested money at a given annual rate of return. ...

For example, the **Rule of 72** states that $1 invested at an annual fixed interest rate of 10% would take 7.2 years ((**72**/10) = 7.2) to grow to $2. In reality, a 10% investment will take 7.3 years to double ((1.107.3 = 2). The Rule of 72 is reasonably accurate for low rates of return.

https://www.investopedia.com/ask/answers/what-is-the-rule-72

SIV: Special Investment Vehicles a similar form of SPV, shadow banking product. Packaging "assets" that are sold and resold to big players like pension investors, life insurance companies, The Fed etc.

SPVs: or SPEs are subsidiary companies (usually LLC) created by a parent company that are protected when the parent goes

Bankrupt. It is used as a funding structure with investors. Another financial "product" of the shadow banking system.

Subprime: **Subprime** borrowers generally have low credit ratings or are people who are perceived of as likely to default on a **loan**.

Resource https://www.investopedia.com/terms/s/subprimeloan.asp

Subprime mortgages would be where the borrowers are rated less than "A" on the rating scale. MBS securities have ratings such as these also .

swag: A slang term used to describe free stuff and giveaways offered by vendors at trade shows to encourage attendees to visit their booth.

Resource : https://www.webopedia.com/TERM/S/swag.html

1099: this is the independent contractor IRS form that is filled out by the Payer and given to the Payee (independent contractor) at the end of the year listing wages paid to them. The IRS gets a copy also.

waver: cannot decide, uncertain; keep changing your mind.

Workers Compensation Insurance: a policy that covers if an employee gets hurt, or injured on the job, the different trades have different rates. Administration being the lowest rates.

SYMBOLS

/ Virgule, means, and/or, I like to use these as you can tell.

RESOURCES

CH. 1

Book, R. Kyosaki *Rich Dad Poor Dad*, Copyright 2017 Plata Publishing; Second edition Scottsdale AZ

CH 2

JohnTrumanWolfe.com March 2020 His Blog *"FINANCIAL Crisis"* "https://johntrumanwolfe.com/category/financial-crisis-2/

Book, R.Kyosaki,*Fake: Fake Money, Fake Teachers, Fake Assets*, 2019 Plata Publishing Scottsdale AZ.

Kyosaki, R. Seidle, *Who stole my Pension?* Copyright 2020 Plata Publishing

Scottsdale AZ

CH3.

Book K. McElroy, *The ABCs of Real Estate Investing* Copyright 2004 Warner Books TWbookmark.com

Book G.Cardone. *How to Create Wealth in Real Estate Investing* Copyright 2018 Cardone Training Tech.,Inc.

Book D. Graziosi *Think a Little Different* Copyright 2004 Think a Little different Mgt. LLC Phoenix AZ

Feb 18, 2008 https://ohmyapt.apartmentratings.com/when_a_registered_sex_offender_lives_near_you.html

CH4.

"ETFs" https://www.wealthsimple.com/en-ca/learn/etfs-vs-stocks N.D.

Book, R.Kyosaki, *Rich dad Poor Dad*, Copyright 2017 Plata Publishing; Second edition Scottsdale AZ

CH 5.

Book, R.Kyosaki, *Fake: Fake Money, Fake Teachers, Fake Assets*, 2019 Plata Publishing Scottsdale AZ https://coinmarketcap.com/currencies N.D.

CH 6.

Grant Cardone,Youtube on *Recessions,Pandemics* https://www.youtube.com/watch?v=EA3ugN7CJm March 20 2020

May 2020 *"Acceptance"* https://grief.com/the-five-stages-of-grief/

"401k" *n.d.* https://www.nerdwallet.com/blog/investing/cashing-out-401k-covid-19/

CH 7.

Book, T. Mello *Home Service Millionaire* Copyright 2018 Home Service Expert Tempe AZ

Book,G. Cardone *The Closer's survival Guide*, Copyright 2009 Card 1 Publications LA CA 90069 Cardone Enterprises Book G. Cardone *Sell or be Sold*, Copyright 2012 Greenleaf Book Group Press

Book, D.Graziosi, *Millionaire Success Habits,* Copyright 2018 Growth Publishing books@growth.com

CH 8.

SBA "PPP" AUG 24 2020 https://www.sba.gov/funding-programs/loans/coronavirus-relief-options/paycheck-protection-program

E. GROVES MAY 1ST 2020 *"BLOG ON CHASE BANK'* https://www.alignable.com/blog/how-small-businesses-can-strike-back-against-this-bank

Wikipedia May 4th 2020 *"TARP Program Bailout"*

https://en.wikipedia.org/wiki/Troubled_Asset_Relief_Program

CH 9.

Article E. Groves *JP Morgan Chase Turns Its Back on Small Business Clients* May 1st 2020

https://www.alignable.com/blog/how-small-businesses-can-strike-back-against-this-bank

TARP PGM WIKIPEDIA */dia.org/wiki/en.wikipeTroubled_Asset_Relief_Program*

Book, R.Kyosaki,*Fake: Fake Money, Fake Teachers, Fake Assets*, 2019 Plata Publishing Scottsdale AZ SECTION on "Shadow Banking"

CH 10.

Wikipedia: references on *Satochi Nakamoto* https://en.wikipedia.org/wiki/Satoshi_Nakamoto

and *White Paper* https://en.wikipedia.org/wiki/White_paper_(disambiguation)

Bitcoin lighting network https://en.wikipedia.org/wiki/Lightning_Network

Oxford dictionary: references on *"blockchain technology"* N.D.

Bankrate.com/ glossary : reference on wallet https://www.bankrate.com/investing/how-to-buy-bitcoins/ N.D.

Bitcoin obituary page; https://news.bitcoin.com/bitcoin-obituaries-records-90-deaths-in-2018/#:~:text=According%20to%20the%20Bitcoin%20Obituaries,grand%20total%20of%20336%20times.

Data.com *comparison value stock market to crypto market cap* N.D.

Ethereumproject.com: references to *Ethereum* N.D.

Bitcoinnews.com: data on *regulations* N.D.

Coinmarketcap.com: references on *value of crypto market* N.D.

CH 11.

R.Kyosaki, R. Seidle, *Who stole my Pension?* Copyright 2020 Plata Publishing

Scottsdale AZ

Book, R.Kyosaki, *Fake: Fake Money, Fake Teachers, Fake Assets*, 2019 Plata Publishing, Scottsdale AZ

G. Cardone Youtube https://www.youtube.com/watch?v=Eub2AzR_E-s April 19 2020

www.ingramcontent.com/pod-product-compliance
Lightning Source LLC
Chambersburg PA
CBHW022042160426
43209CB00002B/41